Let's Start with a Warm-up

Ten Questions about Your Life

What did you dream about in college or in your last year of high school? Have your dreams come true?

Do you have a person who serves as a role model in your life? Have you ever had one? Who is he or she? How did you meet?

What criteria do you use to assess a successful life? What about failures? What is their essence from your point of view?

Which years or events have been or possibly would be the happiest for you – when you want to stop the moment forever?

Do you consider yourself a sociable person? Are you easy to get along with? With whom is it easier for you: with people who are near or who are distant?

Which of your business accomplishments and projects are the most important for you? Do you feel fulfillment in your professional life?

What are your favorite memories? With what are they connected? How do they affect you?

If it would be possible to have been born in another place and time, where and when would you prefer? How, what, or whose life would you want to live?

What is there in your life that you won't be able to complete? What of your beginnings need to be continued and finished by those who will be born later?

What is your favorite motto, metaphor, or symbol of life?

How Young Are You?

How Young Are You?

Understanding
Psychological Age, Time, Causometry
to Create
Meaningful, Harmonious, Productive Lives

A. A. Kronik, Sc.D.

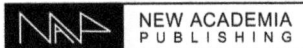

NAP NEW ACADEMIA
PUBLISHING
Washington, DC

New Academia Publishing 2018

Printed in the United States of America

Library of Congress Control Number: 2017943549
ISBN 978-0-9981477-8-9 hardcover (alk. paper)

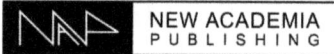

NEW ACADEMIA
PUBLISHING

New Academia Publishing
4401-A Connecticut Ave. NW, #236, Washington DC 20008
info@newacademia.com - www.newacademia.com

For Joseph, the second youngest of twelve brothers, who became an amazing time-oriented dream interpreter more than 3,000 years ago.

Contents

Illustrations

All illustrations are courtesy of the author unless otherwise indicated.

FIGURES

TABLES

Author's Preface

My first contact with psychology came the summer after my sophomore year of high school at a beach near Odessa on the Black Sea. Out of boredom, I read a book called *Psychology as you may like it*. Three months later, my older brother suddenly, and unexpectedly, began to deteriorate from leukemia. He was my pride and joy. In one of our last conversations, he asked me what type of university I intended to enter after graduating from high school. At that time, he was already attending a university and studying history. "If I could do it all over," he said, "I would choose psychology." One year later, instead of him, I entered the Department of Psychology at Kiev University.

I have always been amazed by the concept of age in "the science of the soul," and by the sense of age in my soul. I often forget how old I am. To answer this question, I must ask myself on each occasion the current date, recalling my date of birth, and then doing the arithmetic. The resulting number has very little meaning to me because I, as I always have been, remain younger than my 22-year old brother. Only once in a dream, when I was 28 years old, did I suddenly feel older, and even offer him a bit of advice.

It turned out that nearly every chapter of this book is based on the works indicated in "Sources" (page 113). Unconsciously, I seemed to search for my brother, and over the years, I found him in co-authors who gave me both freedom and understanding while also setting reasonable limits to my sometimes utopian projects. In part that is how this book was born.

This book is one of my steps after our joint international project, *Causometry Study of Psychological Time and Human Life Path: Past, Present and Future*, which won the 2009 Golden Psyche award. I hope, my brother will be proud and could smile with us when we reach the epilogue of this book as well.

The Inner Sense of Age

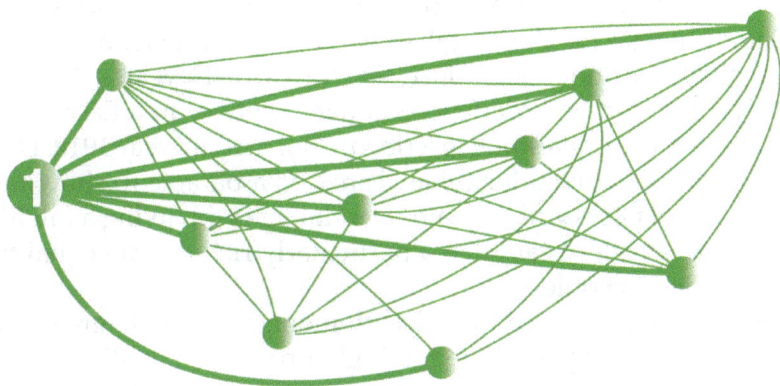

The biblical first man, Adam, supposedly lived for 930 years.[1] Other figures of the Bible were said to have lived for centuries as well. Today, in Abkhazia, (a partially-independent state on the Black Sea), legends tell of 600-year-old brides and 900-year-old grooms.[2] But how long can a person actually live if they avoid sickness, war, or some evil fate?

Gerontologists propose that the natural limit of life is from 100 to 180 years of age[3]. The biblical answer falls well within that range, as well, at "One hundred and twenty years,"[4] which was apparently Moses' age at death.[5]

Moses is said to have lived three thousand years ago. If he lived to 120, would it also be possible for people today? Yes, according to the Guinness Book of World Records. In 2017, the human longevity champion was Jeanne Louise Calment of France, who lived 122 years and 164 days.[6]

Such limits are indeed now possible, though the current average worldwide human lifespan is only about half that age[7]. So how have all centenarians and supercentenarians (who live to 110 and beyond) lived their lives? Do all 100-year-olds live for the same period of time? In other words, can we measure years of life other than by the calendar, or the number of Earthly revolutions around the Sun?

We have found it absolutely necessary to look at our lives both in terms of such measurable time periods, as well as in terms of an individual's "Psychological Age," (that is, a person's experienced lifetime, minus any "lost" or "discarded" years). Life, we have learned, can be experienced either slowly or in a flash. Take, for example, the gravestone inscribed: "Born in the year 1910. Died in the year 1970. Lived for three years," as a parable to show that people do not necessarily equate calendar age with living a full life. Conversely, it is also said that a particularly rich life can equal the lives of several people.

Such a life may be saturated with monetary wealth, great substance, countless experiences, and high intrinsic value. Biographer, Rudolf Balandin, wrote: "To measure the duration of human life in years is the same as estimating a book in pages, a picture in square meters, a sculpture in kilograms. Here the scales are different and the values are other: the achieved, the experienced, and the thought."[8] Therefore, we realize, it is good when people feel their lives have been filled with hundreds of years, no matter where they are along the journey.

So what can we say about people in their thirties, forties, or eighties who realize they are, for example, psychologically, two hundred years old? Does it mean that the more people do and the more intense their lives are, the more profound their thoughts and feelings are? And what of the physical aging process? At forty years old, if a person's psychological age is 100, will the body age more swiftly to correspond to the psychological age?

In fact, the opposite seems to be true. The lives of many artists attest to this: throughout all stages of their lives, and even into old age, many people report feeling (and acting) quite youthful. Let's try to understand this apparent paradox by first looking at how to define age.

How Many Are the Days of Your Life?

We propose that you participate in a mental experiment. Imagine you suddenly learn that the age written on your passport or driver's license is incorrect, and you are uncertain if it indicates you are older or younger than your real, chronological age. Now, as you move through the book, try to rely solely on your inner sense of age to answer the question, "How old are you actually?" You may find, as we did in many experiments, that your "true age" (on official documents) does not necessarily coincide with your inner feeling of age.

We asked eighty-three, highly-educated people, aged twenty-one to forty-four, to participate in the above experiment.[9] Only 24% reported their sense of age to within one year of their actual birth date. Most participants (55%) felt they were younger, while only 21% felt older.

It was fascinating to us that most participants reported feeling younger. Perhaps there is some truth to a comedian's suggestion for regaining his youth. "To become younger, it is necessary to do the following: Simply seize the entire population's watches and calendars and heap them all in a pile on an embankment. As a result, we will then find ourselves without age. Who would know what age we are? Is she 20; is he 40? Who could count?"[10]

It would, of course, be impractical to destroy all the watches, calendars, and dated documents in the world, merely to feel younger. And in fact, it is not necessary. Most people feel younger than they are in reality. Half of those under age thirty in our study felt, on average, four years younger. In the over-thirty population, 73% felt younger by an average of eight years. We also found that the simplest reason people indicated feeling younger was to be flirtatious – the goal being to preserve "eternal youth." Retail sales seem to support this observation; for example, the Ford Motor Company developed a sporty Mustang for a younger generation, but were astonished to discover that people of all ages purchased the car.[11] Economists report that clothing styles designed specifically for young people are in demand by an older age group. Older people who indulge in products and styles associated with youth may preserve a more youthful feeling by doing so.

Yet material goods are only symbols of one age or another. Behavior, words, lifestyle, social norms, and position in society are indicators people use when actually identifying and judging their maturity.

Another factor contributing to one's sense of Psychological Age is the culturally-defined norm for marriage. In the 1960's, American sociologists reported that most people believed men should marry at 20-25 years old, and women at 19-24 years old. A professional career was to begin at 24-26 years old, peak at 45-50 years old, with retirement at 60-65 years old.[12]

Such norms vary, of course, from culture to culture, and generation to generation. But deviations from the norm, as a rule, lead to stressful situations. For example, if a person were to marry very young or very old, he or she would not be following the normal "timetable of life" and could anticipate difficulties. Early marriages were expected to have financial trouble, while late marriages would encounter psychological difficulties.

People would thus be able to sense whether they are young or old by orienting themselves with the accepted age norms for different life events.

Ukrainian sociologist, Natalie Panina, hypothesized that people who have not attained the typical social position in their age group, for example, will feel younger.[13] We tested this supposition by comparing the self-appraised age of married and unmarried people in the former Soviet Union in 1982 (Kiev, Ukraine).[14] At that time, the most common age for Soviet men and women to marry was 23-25 years old.[15] We asked "How does this person feel about himself?" We found that an overwhelming 79% of the unmarried participants felt younger, while 63% of the married people in the same age group felt older. The combination of a person's recorded achievements and social position is considered his or her "social age." But psychologists found that an "internal system of appraisal" is more significant in revealing a person's real sense of age. The same achievement or event is valued differently by every individual, based on his or her perceptions.

For example, two people of the same age, both married at an "appropriate age," may weigh a life event differently; one may believe that sacrificing for family amounts to an achievement, while

the other maintains an independent lifestyle to pursue goals, giving marriage only secondary importance. In the first case, marriage brings immediately perceived "aging," but is less likely to do so in the second case. However, a youthful feeling does not depend on a person's ability to remain socially immature or infantile.

Such egocentric, opinionated, and outspoken people often end up bothering themselves as well as others, and may not actually feel younger than their chronological age because of their distorted views of the future. Furthermore, having a much younger psychological age is not necessarily "better," as we will discuss in more detail.

Towards a New Understanding of Psychological Age

Most of us, at various times in our lives, have wished to be younger and even manifested that desire by behaving immaturely (much to the dismay or embarrassment of those around us). But immaturity is only one characteristic usually associated with being young. There must be some other compelling, and perhaps more mysterious aspect of our youth that has made humanity yearn for a way to stay young or want to relive those blissful childhood days. So what is it about being young that makes us strive to find it again?

To answer that question, we looked at how a person views the future, which has turned out to be more revelatory than how a person views his or her own life history, or how many years a person has lived.

Now, you, too, can figure out your own Psychological Age. More importantly, if you don't like it, and would rather feel younger or older, you can actually change it.

How to Measure Psychological Age

Start by thinking of your Psychological Age as a two-sided scale. On one side is the past and, on the other, the future. When the past outweighs the future (i.e., when you feel that most of the substance of your life and experiences have already occurred) you will feel older than indicated on your driver's license.

Conversely, when the future outweighs the past (i.e. when you

feel that there will be more events ahead of you than behind you) –
you feel younger. We discuss various factors in establishing those
weights. Let us start with a question: "If the total substance of your
life, from birth to death, (including all events and experiences of
the past, present, and future) is 100%, then what percent of that
would you allot to the past? In other words, what percent of your
life substance have you experienced to date?" This is your Index of
Realization (R).

So before reading further, take a few minutes to decide your
R. If it's still not clear, think of it in this way: What percent of your
total expected lifespan have you already realized, by living it?

We have heard many answers to this question ranging from
10%-90%, the average being 41%. So if you haven't stopped to think
how much of your own life has been realized, try again. When
you're done, write your estimated Index of Realization on a note-
pad, then read on.

With some simple arithmetic, you'll be able to get a quick and
rough idea, right now, of your psychological age. You can also get a
more precise number by completing the on-line test (see Figure 1).
Later, we'll guide you through the reasoning of the calculations to
work on changing your Psychological Age.

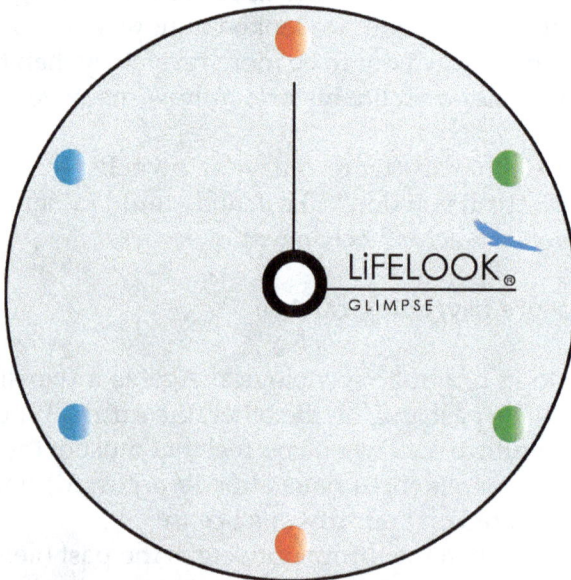

**Figure 1. You can check your psychological age with the on-line test LifeLook®
Glimpse at these websites: www.LifeLook.Net, www.PsychologicalAge.com
and PsychologicalClock.com**

For now, note your estimated Index of Realization (life realized) ____ % = R. Next, write how many years you expect to live _____ = L. Finally, multiply R x L _____ = PA

Here is an example: A person reports that his or her life is only half realized (R=50%) and expects life to last eighty years (L=80), thus has a psychological age of 40 (0.5 x 80). Notice that this calculation is not influenced by the person's chronological age; in fact, we have no idea if this person is 20 or 60 years old. We do know, however, that he or she believes that half the events and experiences of life have already been experienced, but still anticipates the other 50% will occur in the rest of his or her expected lifespan.

Let's say we find two people with a Psychological Age of 40. Kara, who just turned 20, expects to live to 80, but she had such an exciting childhood that she feels she's already realized half of all the things that will ever happen in her lifetime. Her PA of 40 thus makes her 20 years older than her actual chronological age. She might not be pleased at this discovery but knows she can work on changing her psychological age by adjusting her perceptions and attitudes about life.

The second person, Douglas also has a PA of 40. But Douglas was born 60 years ago, and says he's realized merely half of what he believes is possible in his expected 80-year lifespan. In other words, he believes he's going to experience as much in the next 20 years as he did in the previous 60, resulting in him feeling 20 years younger than his chronological age. It is his perception of a full (though potentially overwhelming) future that significantly lowers his PA.

Different Ways of Becoming Younger or Growing Older

People of all ages are often dissatisfied with their age. As children or teens, they want to look and act older. At a mature age, they look back on their youth with nostalgia. While growing older, many people search for remedies to stay youthful or become younger. By understanding your psychological age, you can change your destiny to escape the previously-defined limits of aging. That said, the possibilities are limited. At a young age, your chronological past is too small to be filled with many life experiences. At an old age, most of your reserves for the future have been exhausted. Nevertheless, since you can visit the past or the future in your imagination, you can sometimes successfully outwit chronological age. There are a number of ways to do this.

Epicurus, an ancient Greek philosopher who promoted living a good, pleasurable, and painless life, wrote that, for a man, "As he grows old, he can look back with satisfaction over his past and let the good things he has gained keep him young."[16] Epicurus implies that the man may be trying to compensate psychologically for the biological and social effects of aging. When absorbed by memories of youth, he is making meaningful connections to the present from earlier experiences, and as a result, grows older, but feels younger. A similar rejuvenation can happen when a fatally ill person seeks shelter in past impressions of youth to stave off death.[17]

On the other hand, displacement of one's self into the future may lead a person to self-appraising an older psychological age. A classic example is an immature teenager whose perceived future is overcrowded with plans, projects, and the anticipation of accomplishment. Such people often misjudge the journey they need to take if they are to one day realize their lofty plans.

Another way to look at psychological rejuvenation and aging is to reevaluate the importance of past events. In other words, people can view in the present, a particular childhood moment differently from the way they did while it was happening, or even five years after it occurred. This re-appraisal can reveal previously undetected mistakes or losses with a sense of doom, a feeling of dark clouds rising. At moments like this, a person grows psychologically older, and the past gains significantly more weight in his or her eyes. If a person does not then adopt a fresh attitude towards life, premature psychological aging can occur.

Sometimes, signs of aging can be viewed as an inflated sense of self-importance, an illusion of knowledge, an earlier conservatism, or a skeptical view of the future. In extreme cases, a kind of "personality numbing" results – this is also referred to as a psychological death, where the person seeks to accomplish nothing more and only wants to rest.

As the years go by, it becomes more difficult for most of us to resist the pull of the past. When people get exhausted in one area of activity, the temptation may arise to recapture the pleasures of

youth. Instead, we must search for new activities, be patient, hope, dream, and plan for the future. Goals and plans tend to make a person younger, and not just psychologically. Yugoslavian scientist, R. Savich observed that horticulturists, who are used to waiting years (even decades) to reach their goals of developing new types of plants, actually live longer than people in other occupations.[18] It seems possible, then, that long-term goals not only contribute to people's sense of youth, but increase the duration of their lives as well. Perhaps this makes you stop and wonder if you have enough of your own long-term goals.

While looking to the future is essential, we cannot ignore the sum of our past. Just as the canopy of a tree cannot live without its roots, a personality does not exist without that person's collective life experiences. So if someone completely rejuvenates, his or her past experiences are sent into oblivion, leading to "childhood at a mature age." This would be as undesirable as someone wandering through childhood with the idea that he or she has lived a full life.

The very young has an illusion of a limitless future. However, as the decades pass, this may get replaced with a sense of unfulfilled hopes and self-doubt. To escape such a mid-life crisis, it is good for people to reflect on their accomplishments and respect their past, despite mistakes they may have made. The past is "maturity, reached slowly and against many obstacles, illnesses cured, griefs and despairs overcome, and unconscious risk taken; maturity formed through so many desires, hopes, regrets, forgotten things, loves. A man's age represents a fine cargo of experiences and memories."[19] Thus, we should neither ignore our past, nor constantly pursue it.

But which is better – to feel younger or older than our chronological age? It is natural for teenagers to wish to be older, and older people to be younger. In general, we feel it is best when chronological age and psychological age are not far apart, so that everyone can have a balanced perspective, and fulfilling life experiences.

The Paradoxes of Psychological Time

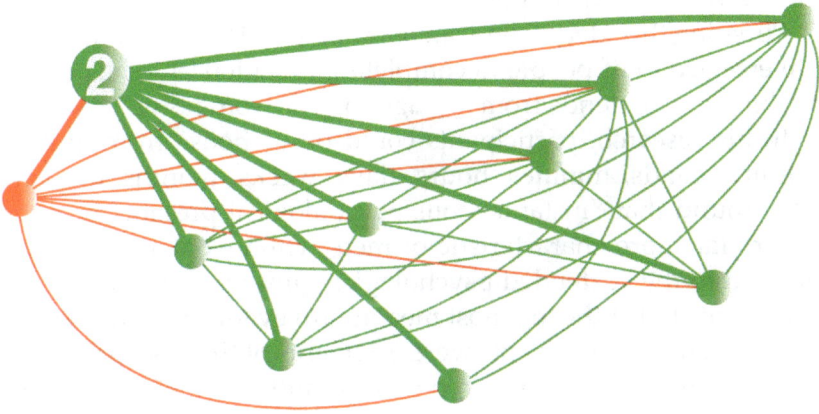

Where is the present located? The answer seems simple and indisputable: between the past and the future. Yet throughout history, esteemed intellectuals such as Aristotle have argued whether the present serves as a partition between "what no longer exists and what does not yet exist,"[20] or if it is what Damascius called an indivisible interval of time, a distinctive quantum.[21]

In contemporary psychology, the concept of "the quantum present" has been firmly established, though researchers view this concept in different ways. For some, the psychological present is a few tenths of a millisecond, in which two stimuli, one following the other, are perceived as one.[22]

For others, the quantum present is equal to the limited time interval in which a person can briefly retain any series of symbols in mind (e.g. a note from a musical composition as an entire configuration). For any sensation, this interval lasts from between two and twelve seconds.[23]

Psychologists also note that boundaries of the present can extend to days, years, or even decades.[24] When writers or actors are asked "What are you working on right now?" for example, most would not respond literally, "I am trying to answer your question." Rather, they would refer to the book or play on which they had been working for months, or even years. Thus, we can see that the range of the "present" is expandable, as are a person's experiences, to extraordinarily vast limits.

Pursuing this idea, American psychologist Thomas Cottle asked a diverse group of people to complete this sentence: "The present, as I think of it, extends from ___ ago to ____ from now."

In his research, participants could only choose from units of time in seconds, minutes, hours, days, weeks, months, or years. Cottle found that "instantaneous psychological present" responses were far more characteristic of men, while women were more disposed to the "extended psychological present."[25] He also asked participants to list the ten most meaningful events in their lifetimes and to specify if these events were fragments of the past, present, or future. As expected, women reported far more events in the "present" than did men.

There is one matter, however, on which most psychologists concur, that, to some extent, the present is part of an interval of physical time that exists. This interval serves as a kind of receptacle for events that a person experiences as the present, which is followed by the future and preceded by the past. Think of it like a raft floating down a river from its source to its mouth, and all the adventures it encounters which occur along its surface. Anything that lingers in the river after the raft has gone by is out of the bounds of the present, and consists merely of memories; anything ahead of it can only be hope.

Yet, this perspective of physical time has been questioned more than once. Marietta Shaginian remarked, "How often in my life has the past collided with today's or even tomorrow's days! Is time really divided into yesterday, today, and tomorrow?"[26] Social anthropologists also doubt the single notion of linear time. They point to the Hopi Indian tribe, for whom the idea of a present that appears between a past and future is entirely foreign.[27]

In mythological consciousness, the past and the future often coexist within the present so that it is possible to communicate with the deceased, or even to see the future in great detail. This is exem-

plified by the assembly of deceased chiefs and heroes who were said to often intervene in world matters, and by spirits or prophets who were said to consult ancient people when they struggled with weighty decisions. Whatever the connection between the human past and the future, it seems to be more than a linear relationship.

Perhaps, though, examples of ancient people and culture no longer apply to our modern society. Some say that time is experienced differently today: "There is only a moment between past and future, just it is called the Life,"[28] whether it is seconds or years. So why are past events, even dreams and expectations – all far removed from daily reality – sometimes more vital and substantive than day-to-day life?

Psychological Time and Personality, a Study[29]

To understand the power of the past in the present of human lives, we asked forty-five engineers, ages 22-32, to identify the ten most significant (and relatively instantaneous) events in their lives, even if the events had not yet occurred. This research was similar to the Cottle study, except our participants were asked to use their own perceptions of time: to put the events in chronological order (by month and year) and to indicate past, present, or future.

They placed, on average, 3 of 10 events in the present. But only half the participants placed present events in chronological sequence. The other half "sprinkled" present events between past and future ones. As a result, the present was scattered between other events not designated as the present. We called this "the phenomenon of the partial present," as it takes place when portions of the present can be found anywhere on the chronological axis. Some participants placed what they referred to as present time events many years prior to the actual research time period, while past and future events were placed closer to the date (Sept. 1982) of the study we were conducting .

One participant divided his life's ten most significant events into the past (P), present (PR), and future (F). In his interpretation, the quantum present does not exist either (see Figure 2).

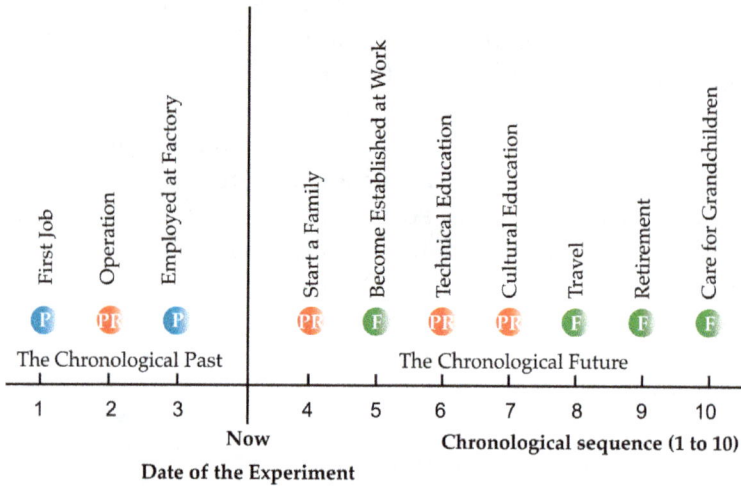

Figure 2. The phenomenon of the partial present.

Note the paradox in his time appraisal, with a present event (2) preceding a past one (3), and a future event (5) preceding the present (6 and 7). When the present gets separated into three isolated parts, no notion of the quantum present, which requires sequence, seems to apply.

In another experiment, participants were asked to first write specific dates of events, then to categorize them as the past, present, or future. Even with the structured guidance to place events in chronological order, the phenomenon of the partial present remained.

The paradox of psychological time has long been a compelling issue to philosophers and poets. Goethe wrote, "That I possess, seems far away to me. And what is gone becomes reality."[30]

Why Are Events Experienced as the Present?

In the seventeenth century, German philosopher Gottfried Leibniz speculated about the connection between time and cause-effect relationships.[31] Many scientists believed that the answer to the question, "Which of two events occurred first and which second?" only

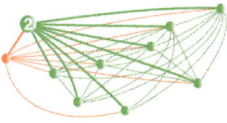

required knowing which event was the cause and which the effect. Since cause always precedes effect, the solution appeared easy. However, this simplistic explanation failed to account for many other, and quite different conceptions of the nature of time.

The causal concept of time still has quite a few supporters, including physicists, some philosophers, and cultural historians. "Can we imagine what our familiar idea of time would be, if we were not accustomed to considering phenomena as bound together in the relation of cause and effect?" wrote French ethnographer and psychologist, Lucien Levy Bruhl[32] in 1923. Russian scientists, such as Aleksei Losev[33], Olga Freidenberg[34], Dmitrii Likhachev[35], Mikhail Steblin-Kamenskii[36], and Aaron Gurevich[37] concur that events which temporarily remain in order, spring up in life, based on the realization of their causal connections.

Indeed, in our daily lives, we often use cause-effect or goal-driven language such as "because of that," "for the purpose of," "I took vacation time so that I could visit my mother," or "I got married because I fell in love."

Some connections are linked by events realized in the past, and thus are already part of a person's life experience. When parents teach a child by example ("I became a successful engineer because I studied very hard in school"), they refer to past experience. Adding, "If you study hard, then you will be able to attend a university," they create in the child's mind, a cause-effect link to the future. We call these types of chronological connections "potential," the most critical being from the past to the future. Thus, "realized" connections belong to the past, to the world of memory. "Potential" connections belong to the world of reverie and fantasy in a possible future. "Actual" connections validate the existence of a psychological present, not a mere instant of time, but a bridge between the past and the future, as life itself.

Sometimes, though, the past occupies only a modest place in a person's life, such as for a university student concentrating on graduation and getting a job.[38] In Figure 3, we see that all of the person's selected events, tied to present efforts and hopes, are found in the future.

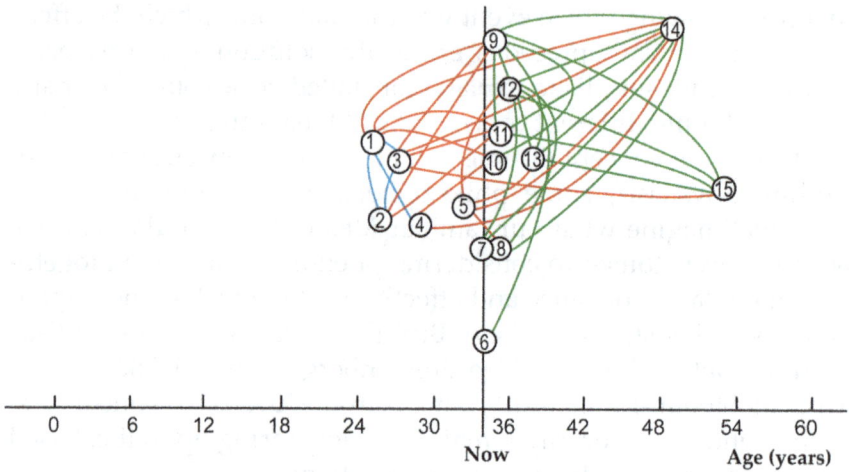

Figure 3. Example of a graph of realized (blue), actual (red) and potential (green) connections between life's events (a man, age 34). List of his life events: (1) marriage; (2) work in an editorial office; (3) entering university; (4) child's birth; (5) acquaintance; (6) hike; (7) wife's post-graduate; (8) obtaining a room; (9) graduation; (10) studies with a child; (11) creative work; (12) even temper; (13) change place of residence; (14) creative work with wife and child; (15) welfare of the family.

Psychologists have long known of "the effect of unfinished tasks,"[39] where we are tormented by a dreadful feeling because of actions that were started but never finished. This feeling always lives inside us in the present time.

Let's say two people watch a TV movie. After a week, one of them may forget it, though the other may anxiously await the sequel. Months later, the two people are asked to categorize the movie screening as a past or future event. Their answers will be different. One of them will place the event in the past. But chances are that the other person (the one awaiting the sequel) will place it in the present.

We conducted further research to investigate this phenomenon[40]. This time, we pre-determined ten significant life events: 1) First love, 2) The most important meeting in life, 3) Changing jobs, 4) Graduating from college, 5) Birth of first child, 6) Profound disappointment, 7) Purchasing a house, 8) Marriage, 9) Promotion at work, and 10) Getting a first job.

We asked participants to sequence the events, to identify possible cause-effect and goal-determined connections between these events, to count "actual," "potential," and "realized" connections for each event, and to determine the "degree of actuality" (i.e. closeness to the present moment) for each event.

As expected, the importance that a person attributed to events in the present proved to be greater than that of past or future events. For example, most participants found "Graduation from college" and "First job" to be the most actual, the most present. They consistently set "First love" and "Birth of first child" in the past, but "Changing jobs," "Promotion," and "Purchasing a house" in the future.

Thus, if we delve deeper, attempt to clearly understand the results of the experiment, and try to create a new perspective, we may learn to control time – or at least – our personal feelings about time.

Is It Possible to Stop an Instant?

Aristippus, one of Socrates' students, wrote, "Only the present is truly ours."[41] He offers advice to seize the moment, for it will last but an instant. This idea of maximizing pleasure every moment of life (as Epicuras also advocated) is only possible, however, if people know how to do so, and view life as the combination of endless instants of the present.

Another school of thought, such as the one expressed by eighteenth century French romanticist Joseph Joubert, is that "We should treat our life as we treat writings: see that the beginning, the middle, and the end are in proportion – in harmony."[42]

Identifiable relationships between the past, present, and future allow us to extend an instant in the present, by reintegrating the past and future into this moment in time. In so doing, we are not experiencing a series of distinct instants, but rather one, longer moment, thanks to our ability to reference our past, and imagine our future. In other words, to not forget, anticipate the future. To attain your goals, turn to the past. If you are afraid to look into the eyes of the future, you will not be able to see the present. If you can understand the past, you can fill the present.

The Amazing Potential of Psychological Time to Contract and Suspend: What Makes a Good Watch?

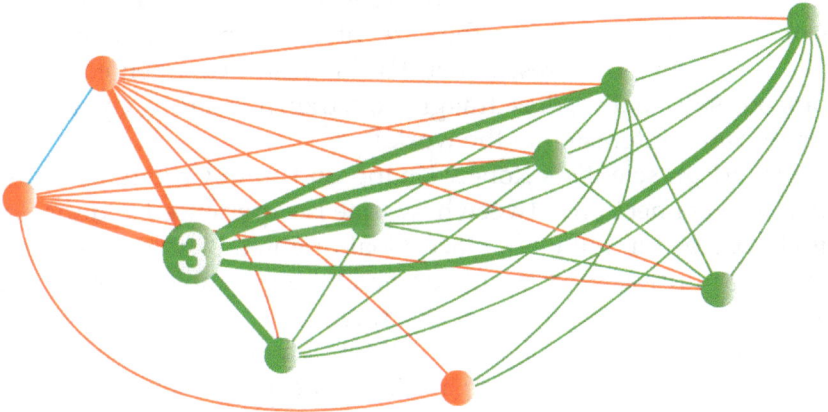

A good watch should undeniably keep exact time. It should not stop an hour before a scheduled meeting, nor have its hands randomly speed up or slow down. It is impartially accurate, regardless of whether its owner is a child or an adult, happy or sad, working or sleeping.

We need accurate watches precisely because we, humans, are not impartial when it comes to measuring the passage of time. In fact, when we're not wishing it would just speed along or stop, we may lose track of it altogether.

Students in a lecture glance frequently at their watches or phones, surprised at how slowly the minutes are passing, and even check with others around them to see if their timepieces are functioning properly. An early twentieth-century way to explain the concept of relativity was to imagine that "an hour sitting with a pretty girl on a park bench passes like a minute, but a minute sitting on a hot stove seems like an hour."[43] We humans simply do not perceive time the same way as each other, or even the same as we, ourselves experienced it in the same setting at a later date.

Scientist Georgii Borisovskii[44] asked participants to listen and to estimate the running time for two performances of the opera "Prophet" by Rimsky-Korsakoff: one by little-known Petrov and one by world-renowned Chaliapin. All the listeners guessed close to the elapsed time for Petrov's version but grossly over-estimated the length of Chaliapin's. Time seems to progress slowly when people are bored, but when they are interested in the task at hand, time speeds by. Time researcher, Paul Fraisse, commented that if someone says that work is dragging on, then it is safe to say that the person is not interested in the work.[45]

American scientists Robert Knapp and John Garbutt also discovered a connection between how time is experienced and the desire to succeed in the work place. Goal-oriented people experience time as compressed, fast, and strained.[46] Such people refer to time as "a fast-moving shuttle," "a speeding train," "a galloping horseman," "a bird in flight," "a fleeing thief," "a dashing waterfall," or "a whirligig." When workers are less concerned about success or goals, they describe time as "a vast expanse of sky," "a quiet, motionless ocean," "a stairway leading upward," or "a road leading over a hill."[47]

Psychological time not only appears to speed up and slow down; it can also be perceived as fragmented. For example, Hamlet said: "The time is out of joint. O cursed spite that ever I was born to set it right!"[48] People can experience sharp tears in time. Moscow scientists Natalia Bragina and Tatiana Dobrokhotova found that people with right-brain damage seem to have the power to stop, or tear time.[49]

Author Daniil Granin wrote, "The time in this room has never moved this slowly. The time has been stretched and torn into little events, and in the middle of this process, time has stopped."[50] This experience of torn time is reported to feel like stagnation or deadlock, as opposed to an even and tightly-woven, normal fabric of time. Where the fabric of time is intact, there are strong connections between the past, present, and future.

Timepieces and measurements of the Earth's movements today are so accurate that we not only know we have to add a leap year

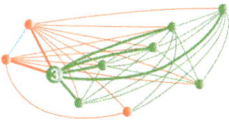

every fourth year, we can also add a "leap second" to atomic clocks when needed to adjust for occasional irregularities in the Earth's rotation. Such precision is a great accomplishment. But can we create a watch capable of measuring human psychological time? Although a practical answer to this question will probably not be found in the immediate future, the most basic principles for a solution may already appear in psychological research.

Why Does Time Contract?

Immanuel Kant, an eighteenth century German philosopher, was the first to propose the notion that the more events a person experiences during an interval of time, the more prolonged the interval seems, in retrospect.[51] Nineteenth century French philosopher Jean-Marie Guyau suggested using the number of perceived events to evaluate the psychological duration of time. He felt that only this could explain the mysteries of time (such as how numerous events can be experienced in a dream in only seconds, while in reality, these events would take hours or even days).[52]

With the progress of experimental psychology, we see examples of Kant's "event-related" explanation in contrast to Guyau's views. For example, people estimate "full" minutes of their lives (time periods filled with many, many events) to last longer than "hollow" minutes (time periods with few or no events). So when weeks, months, or years are "full" – then time seems to progress quickly. There is great disparity between perceived evaluation and brief segments of chronological time.

An observation by nineteenth century American psychologist William James expands this theme: "In general, a time filled with varied and interesting experiences seems short in passing, but long, as we look back. On the other hand, a track of time empty of experiences seems long in passing, but in retrospect, short."[53]

Why is this? It is important to keep in mind the three types of connections: realized (connections between events in the chronological past), potential (connections between events in the chronological future), and actual (connections linking the past to the future). The number of connections that a person creates between life events tells us that person's perspective on the experience, and where it resides in his or her psychological time.

Naturally, people can see the same life events differently and will make connections to different parts of their psychological time. Suppose that two people, admitted to the same college, graduated together, and began working at the same time. Both were driven to build an important invention and, as a result, were promoted at work.

One person may feel that everything in life will happen by itself – that the next event will follow sequentially from the previous one. This is the peculiar logic of "the escalator of life;" it is enough that you get on the first step and the rest of your upward mobility is guaranteed.

The other person believes that to attain true success, considerable effort has to be made "for the purpose of" forward momentum. Having decided as a child to invent something someday, the second person consciously chose to attend a specialized college, seek out a particular job, and move up the professional ladder.

So how did these two people experience time, and what differentiates their impressions of the events? First, there is a large difference in the number of actual connections they report between the same events. The first person only made one "actual" connection, which was between "begin working" and "create an invention." All other connections were "realized" or "potential." The second person considered all five events, more or less, to be actual. As we observed, the greater the number of "actual" connections, the closer they revolve around the person's psychological "immediate time." As a result, the past remains not far from the present, and the future approaches rapidly—shrinking time in a person's experience.

In contrast, the less actual the events, the farther they drift into the past, and the further away they seem in the distant future (thus expanding time). In other words, when a person reports few "actual" connections, time is expanded, as for the person on the escalator. With a myriad actual connections, time is contracted, as for the second person.

However, both individuals are capable of re-evaluating their perceptions of events and re-considering the connections they make between the past, present, and future. They can then make fewer or greater actual, realized, and potential connections, alternatively expanding or contracting time, as desired.

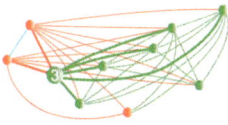

We tested this hypothesis in an experiment,[54] this time asking participants to list the fifteen most meaningful events of their lifetime. We then asked them to arrange these events in chronological order and to indicate if they were linked by cause-effect or goal-oriented connections. Finally, they were asked to evaluate their experience of time on a scale ranging from "compressed" to "expanded."

As expected, the participants who evaluated time as compressed had a greater number of actual connections than the participants who evaluated time as expanded. On the whole, time was most often experienced as compressed, though particularly so with men, who had more "actual" connections than women.

When psychological time is maximally compressed, the past and the future cease to exist for the person experiencing it. Everything seems to occur in the present. As a result, anticipated events converge to such an extent that they hold the illusion of reality. This potentially dangerous illusion can provoke premature actions. Psychologist Kurt Lewin described a legal case in which several prisoners, after being informed of their impending and early release from prison for good behavior, surprisingly attempted to escape just a few days prior to their scheduled release.[55] A multitude of new actual connections was formulated in the minds of the prisoners. Their imminent release from prison was experienced as the "immediate present," resulting in maximally compressed time, and the completion of untimely, and unfortunate actions.

If the mechanism for experiencing time were better understood, we believe that it could be better controlled. We can currently help many people experiencing stress, for example, to reduce tension by deliberately distracting themselves from "empty" thoughts. Other methods for guided thought are also available to experience time differently, as humans have recognized discomfort when time seems to ruthlessly drag out. The Dhammapada says, "Those who are slaves to passions follow the stream (of craving), as a spider the web that he has made himself. Wise people, when they have cut this (craving), leave the world, free from cares, leaving all sorrow behind."[56]

People need compressed time. It is possible to fill time with actual events and connections. "Time is action," wrote Nikolai Rerikh, "time is thought... if we consider the veritable importance of humankind; time needs to be, first and foremost, wonderfully full."[57]

Nevertheless, along this tense path, a person may run into danger if his or her consciousness is completely absorbed by actual connections, but void of realized or potential connections. The situation is labeled "combustion." This is when a person's mind is totally absorbed by daily activities thought to be immediately necessary. In this condition, a person does not entertain any future events not entirely prepared in the thoughts and actions of the past, even to the point of rejecting dreams and fantasies. Moreover, the person seems to entirely forget the past. Only causes and remedies of future events are visible.

Excessively compressed and strained time is characterized by energetic activities and a full present. The person feels unable to stop an instant, even to glance back or casually ponder. But people need, at least occasionally, to think back to actions and decisions, and to analyze and learn from previous occurrences. Otherwise, they risk falling into the "topical interest" trap, in which they may always experience time difficulties, no matter how much time is available in reality.

Memories and dreams, however, can release the grip of time, saturating an event with realized and potential connections, optimizing it and ultimately allowing time to expand and enhance a person's experience.

A Thread Connecting Time

Cottle observed such "interrupted time" when he asked a group of participants to use three circles and sketch on paper their personal comprehension of the past, present, and future.[58] The circles touched, intersected, or engulfed each other. Both small and large interruptions in psychological time were displayed. Many participants drew an "atomic" picture – when circles were separately arranged and completely isolated. These results were corroborated by our research using the same methods. Clearly, the strings of time are not torn only for Hamlet. What stands behind the metaphor? What enables time to be experienced as torn or interrupted?

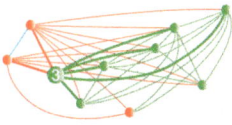

It is easy to identify an interrupted state with a fixed spatial shape using broken lines, profoundly rupturing otherwise smooth boundaries. Take, for example, a road (leading to the horizon) that appears to be continuous. If the end of the road is visible, but after the road ends, there is an open field through which no one has passed, it leaves the impression of broken space.

Time also consists of distinctive "routes" between events. The routes can be lengthy and connect chronologically remote events, or short, linking proximate events. The mechanism of interruption we observed is that the shorter the chronological length of actual connections between events, the more that time is experienced as broken.

So does one event serve as the cause or the goal for the other? Improbable connections are similar to an unexplored path. Highly probable connections are similar to a well-traveled road. If the two roads are equal in length, then the continuous road will seemingly have fewer obstacles interrupting the path. Therefore, to understand the nature of interrupted time, it is essential not only to consider the length of the connection but also the certainty of the interruption's existence.

Time is experienced as uninterrupted by people who are certain that their life events of the distant past are connected to those of the distant future. For such people, actual connections of the present extend for years and decades. If these connections are brief, and a person has doubts about them, then time will be torn and a sequence of "adventurous" events will not be linked together.

To verify this supposition, we asked participants to evaluate their experience of time using a scale that was labeled "interrupted" on one end and "uninterrupted" on the other. The disparity in responses was astonishing. The average length of actual connections for uninterrupted time was twenty-five years, but only sixteen for interrupted time. Nevertheless, even with the shorter period, a person cannot be entirely sure whether a past event serves as the cause of or a solution for reaching the future.[59]

People with different personality types (strategists, tacticians, and operationalists)[60] link life events differently. Strategists attain the greatest degree of success by coordinating their actions with long-term prospects; therefore, they link distant events, think concretely and exuberantly, and experience time as uninterrupted. Life is one long highway. Operationalists attempt to fully understand the cause of a situation, even to the point of sacrificing the ability to cope with it. To them, life amounts to several small, tangled, intricate, and interrupted paths. Tacticians, the majority of the population, are interested in interim situations; to them, life is made up of constantly changing roads.

So if you wanted to restore connections and feel that time was less interrupted, you could, for example, delay some planned events in your life. Alternatively, you could move more carefully toward goals, so as not to move too hastily, especially if you have not yet understood the psychological time connections between recent achievements and past ones.

You could also create new and distant goals, realizing the distant consequences of present-day actions, and remembering that in the remote, almost forgotten past are still possible remedies for future events. By engaging in such activity, you can make strong and lengthy actual connections to establish uninterrupted psychological time. The highest form of uninterruption is the feeling of time's continuity, where causes and results are seen beyond your personal biological boundaries—in both historical past and future.

It is remarkable to be able to remove significant life events from your own boundaries to the extent that, from your own point of view, you do not perceive your birth as the beginning of life's path, nor do you see death as the end. Rather, you view your major life events as occurring throughout preceding and succeeding generations.

The substance of historical events will vary from person to person. For one, it might be actions and legacies of ancestors, or accomplishments of children and grandchildren. For another, it might be famous people from the past and thankful memories of a generation. In both cases, understanding the historical scale of a person's life broadens and saturates each one's sense of psychological time. The connected events, sometimes divided by centuries, serve to make cultural and social meaning from ideas, actions, and behavior. In truly uninterrupted connections, the event of your own death does not even interrupt your psychological time.

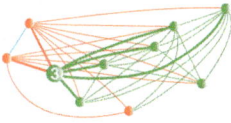

To reiterate, despite the fact that death moves closer each second, each hour, each year, time can still be experienced as unbroken. In fact, as people age, research shows that with the transition from youth to maturity, they have less of an egocentric concept of time, and move towards a growing sense of responsibility for future generations towards a more history-centric concept of time.[61]

If a watch could be invented to measure both stretched and torn psychological time, as we wished earlier, it would have to assess our personal comprehension of time, our perceptions of cause and effect, goals, and solutions. To also display the future, it would have to internally calculate our past, present, and future psychological connections into a technological manifestation of psychological time on a clock face. We welcome replies to this challenge.

The Trips to Long Ago and
Not Very Soon

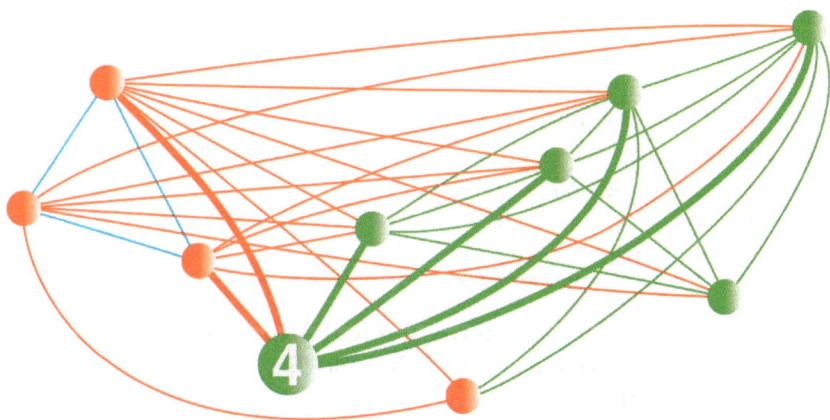

Do ancient events always take place earlier than more recent events? If we listen closely to ourselves, this question is not rhetorical. Parents might say to their child who was playing that she was supposed to go to sleep "a long time ago." However, if the child asked to have the parents read yesterday's bedtime story, they would be surprised and say that the child had already heard the story "not too long ago."

The resulting confusion can occur when a series of events does not seem to correspond with chronological time. We called it an "inversion" of the evaluation of distance in time. These non-conforming cases occur often when evaluating future events. For example, when you make a date for Friday night, you might say, "See you soon," but it's Tuesday, and you feel that the end of the working day will not at all be "soon."

You can find your own inversions, too. List 10-15 events from your life (work, school, family, friends, nature, society, and inner life). Include events from the past and future. Then estimate, to the best of your ability, the distance from this very moment to the real or expected date of each event, using the distance scale in Table 1.

Table 1. The scale of subjective temporal distance.

+5	not soon at all
+4	not soon
+3	not very soon
+2	soon
+1	very soon
0	now
-1	not at all long ago
-2	not long ago
-3	not very long ago
-4	long ago
-5	very long ago

Next to your estimates, write the real or planned dates of each event, and you may discover considerable disparities between your perceptions and the actual dates.

Similar experiments have shown that the inversion of temporal distance is a common occurrence. For every six or seven inversions experienced by men , women have ten or eleven. Furthermore, the order of past events was disturbed twice as frequently as that of future ones.[62]

This evaluation of time is frequently experienced by people with an artistic or humanitarian bent and prone to dreaming or deep reflection about their lives. For these people, 30-35% inversion is normal. More rational, technically knowledgeable people reported less frequent inversions, though they were still subject to the sense that decades-old events do not seem so old, while events that took place months ago seem very far away indeed.

Furthermore, people seemed to have different time experiences with unpleasant events than with pleasant ones. Freud said that, "the essence of repression lies simply in turning away, and keeping it at a distance, from the conscious."[63] Research shows that people remember 43% of pleasant events and only 28% of unpleasant ones.[64]

Similarly, with future events, people displayed "unrealistic optimism."[65] They were inclined to think that pleasant events would

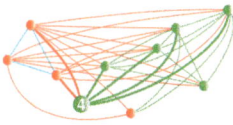

be more probable in their own lives. Conversely, unpleasant events would be less probable; in general, they felt "lucky."

Yet in a follow-up, we asked people to specifically identify pleasant and unpleasant events from their past and future, and to place them on the "very long ago" to "not soon at all" timeline. Both categories of events were arranged identically in the psychological past and future. Why? It seems that repressed events and their distance in time are different phenomena. In the first case, the events completely "fell" from time. In the second case, the events were more or less part of the remote past or future. It appears that the psychological mechanism of repression is not related to the inversion of distance.

I Am Here, but When?

Thanks to the "hypnotic miracle"[66] over a hundred years ago, a twenty-nine-year-old woman was hypnotized to believe she was just seven years old. When asked to write her name, she did so slowly, precisely, making mistakes, and writing in a child's handwriting. Later, the suggested age was two and a half years old. The hypnotized woman sat on the floor and played with an imaginary doll. Repeatedly, she was transported to other moments in her life: five, six, seven, eight, ten, fifteen, and twenty years old. The phenomenon is called "hypnotic regression of age." This condition can be brought out in people having a high level of suggestibility as well as in people having good mental and psychological health.[67]

Indeed, the past does live within us. And the future? Is the future also within us? Can we persuade a person that he or she is older than in reality? Would a person behave under hypnosis as he or she would in years to come? Under hypnosis a person's "self" (which has been displaced into the past or future) can be stable, even in different types of personalities: those living in the past (characteristically emotional and depressed), in the present (impulsive and sensitive), or in the future (enterprising).[68] To become future-oriented, is to be confident in one's own personal strength and to behave as "master of your own destiny." It is not by chance that after successful psychotherapy, it is possible for a person to transform from being "past-oriented" to being "future-oriented."[69]

Given the chance to self-identify as living with a personal time center in the past, present or future, 47% of the participants attributed themselves to an interval between the chronological past and future. Another 25% sat squarely in the chronological past, while 28% located their time center between events of the chronological future. Men most often placed themselves in the future and women in the past. As Oscar Wilde said, "I like men who have a future, and women who have a past."[70]

People's thoughts often return to the past or jump to the future, but they are linked closely to the present by relatives and loved ones.[71] For people whose psychological "now" coincided best with the chronological "now," half their personal interactions were categorized as close ("together") relationships.

For those whose self was displaced to the past, only 28% of their relationships were "together," while 52% were "separated." For people in the psychological future, 15% of their relationships were "together" and 62% were "separated." This indicated that the more relationships in the chronological present, the more difficult it is to break free from this point in time. We speculate that perhaps people with close relationships have no need to leap into the past or future. Vladimir Vysotsky concurs:[72]

I love you now
It's not a secret or for show
Not "before" and not "after"
Burning in your light
Crying or laughing
But I love you right now
In the past – I don't want
In the future – I don't know

Surely, for many people, "living in the past" is tantamount to lost friends and lovers. "Living in the future" may be an escape from loneliness today, in hopes of finding someone tomorrow. A person who lives in the present is sensitive to the feelings and moods of others. Those stranded in the past have an immense anchor of inertia and are accustomed to bearing the burdens of memory. When running ahead to the future, a person often does not appreciate what is available today.

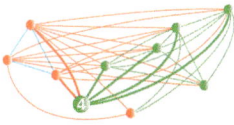

How Can Memories and Silent Dreams Be Awakened?

The brief displacement of the self in time happens regularly. Transformations from distant past to future are called "time decentering," as illustrated in the phrase, "that is what I expected," or "I will remember that." They appear in vivid memories of love as well as in thoughts of death, such as "I met you, and all the past // Reviving in my dying heart."[73] Emile Zola so vividly imagined the scene of his own death that, on occasion, his nightmares awakened him.[74]

By decentering, people can see their path of life in a volumetric and panoramic way; they can understand every event from different positions in time, human culture, history, past and future generations. Notably, decentering leads to miraculous transformation of the psychological past, present, and future. It radically changes the shape and appearance of connections between events. (Remember that realized connections link events of the chronological past, potential connections link future events, and actual connections link the past with the future).

These connections are the units of psychological time – able to transform from one to another. Thus, connections regarded as actual in the chronological present can be experienced as realized if a person looks at them from the future:

Young people!
For your future memories
Please carefully draw your current picture.
Pin-hsin[75]

Actual connections transform into potential if a person lives in the past, not noticing that his or her expectations and fears are already happening. Realized connections are freshly becoming actual, or possibly experienced as potential if a person remains in the distant past. Additionally, in the moment of dreaming and hoping, potential connections become actual and transform from the psychological future into the psychological present.

These unusual transformations were found in psychologically unhealthy patients whose right side of the brain was not functioning properly.[76] One person felt he had already experienced a situation even though he had not (déjà vu, i. e. as "already visible," "already experienced" in the past.)[77]

Ivan Goncharov wrote in *Oblomov*, that

> In rare instances there come to a man fleeting moments of abstraction when he seems to be reliving past stages of his life. Whether he has previously beheld in sleep the phenomena which are passing before his vision, or whether he has gone through a previous existence and has since forgotten it, we cannot say; but at all events he can see the same persons around him as were present in the first instance, and hear the same words as were uttered then.[78]

Instant experiences (when under the influence of the electrical stimulation of a human's brain, a person again experiences fragments of the past) are similar to the enticement of the "stream of consciousness." A person is enticed when delving deeply into the world of memories and may completely renounce all interests of today. However, a healthy adult self, if located in the past or the future can return to the chronological present with ease. With psychological trouble, this return is difficult. The result is an unusual stagnation of many feelings and a disengagement from current reality.

A person can shift the self in time with relative success. At a very young age, it is hard to understand the basic concept of tomorrow. From age eleven to thirteen, Bradley, Oakden and Sturt found that a child can grasp the idea of the historical past.[79] To build a perspective of the future, however, one needs a high level of intelligence. Even high school students, with strong aspirations for the future, comprehend the future as amorphous.

It is also possible to develop the skills to analyze your individual personal life from "different points in time." To start, imagine that present time is something that is expected; then view, from the future, events that are already past. After a few similar expeditions, a person's picture of life becomes clearer, richer, and possibly even more real. All energy is concentrated in the present, potentially giving a person new vigor to solve actual problems.

When, as adults, we remember our childhood, it seems ex-

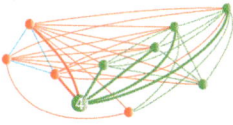

tremely distant. However, when a person reverts to childhood, it seems very close. Active speculation about the future is also necessary. An inquiry was conducted by the International Institute of World Problems in the 1970's[80] as to how far away the year 2000 seemed. It was much closer for individuals from socialist and third world countries than for those from industrialized and capitalist countries. Overall, the year 2000 was closest for individuals from a high social stratum.

Using the phrases "a long time ago," "not so long ago," "now," and "soon" – our own psychological time is speaking to us, and we should listen. These experiences can release powerful and energetic charges that can stimulate us to reach our goals. A person's past is then perceived as a springboard for the realization of future goals. Even if it is understood that perhaps years or even decades separate us from success, we can still feel the closeness of our desires, and may be confident that they will be realized soon. The sense of too much distance can leave a person unmotivated, with the feeling that the future will not be here soon, so he or she fails to carry out actions. "Not very soon" suddenly transforms into merely a situation that "could happen."

That which motivates a person's perception of the future does so for the past as well. By reviewing past events as they affect the future, a person realizes the consequences of actions. Events that occurred years ago can be perceived as occurring right now, or not so long ago, and can help a person not be bogged down by the rush of daily life. On the other hand, by cutting all connections from the past to the future, it is possible to begin life anew, to completely dismiss the past, and to bury a former self. As a result, all events from the past seem very long ago, with no turning back.

What Makes for Creative Longevity?

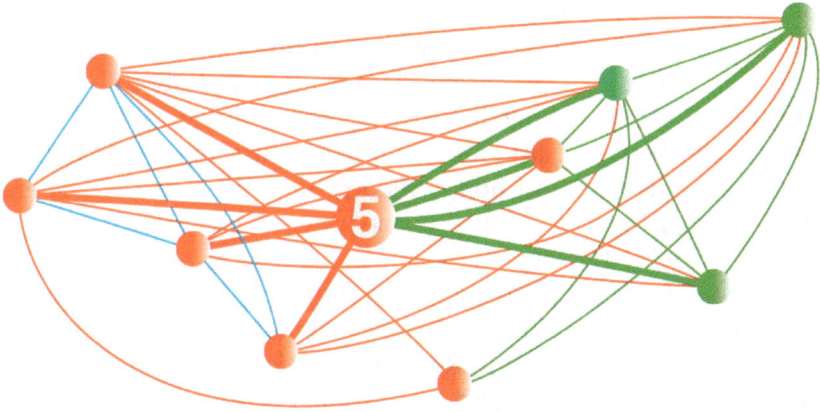

Life is a slope. As long as you're going up, you're looking towards the top and you feel happy; but when you reach it, suddenly you can see the road going downhill...

Maupassant[81]

As a rule, between the ages of 25-30, people's senses, memory, and intellect are at their highest point, then slowly dissipate.[82] In the 1960's, psychologist Harvey Lehman found that the height of creative achievement for physicists, chemists, and mathematicians was around 30, while for biologists and humanitarians it was around age 40, with only a small splash of activity as a last surge between ages 55-60.[83] And yet, many exceptions exist.

For example, when Paul Hamory, who placed high in the Swiss fencing championship, was asked by reporters how he performed so well at age eighty-two, he answered that he was willing to discuss any topic, except his age. "I participate in sports," he declared, "so that I can ignore my birth date." Likewise, ninety-year-old literary critic Viktor Shklovskiy commented that the secret to creative longevity was that self-confidence and impertinence do not depend on age and circumstance.[84] In fact, a creative person can preserve his or her youthful qualities and way of thinking well into old age.[85]

How Can Life Productivity Be Evaluated?

The simplest way to evaluate life is by length. However, long life only gains meaning and value when it is filled with valuable contents. The words of *The Dhammapada* can be said about a person who squanders his or her life away without a use for self or for others: "A man is not an elder simply because his head (hair) is grey. His age is ripe, but he is called grown old in vain."[86] Therefore, length or "working time" is one index of life, and richness or "productivity" is another.

Results of our research[87] revealed that people evaluate the significance of events according to how events influence their lives, goals, and yet other events. Research participants were asked to analyze their life course and assess each five-year period (past through future) using a concentration of significant events (1 = smallest degree of concentration of events, 10 = maximum concentration of events).

The portrait of life, "ascent...peak...descent," about which Maupassant[88] wrote, best describes our results, though the age of people at their peak varied. Young engineers in their first year of work pessimistically viewed a continuous reduction of life events after peaking at age 20 (perhaps due to a difficult time adapting to conditions of independent life). People over 28 most often saw their peak in the past, while high school seniors saw their peak in the near future, between 20-25 years of age.

In Search of a Vocation

The psychological age of students is one of the most interesting indexes of the picture of life. The greater the specific weight of the future, the younger a person feels. The greater the weight of the past, the older the self-evaluation. Students (270 total) were divided into three groups: the first (36%) with a psychological age higher than their chronological age ("older"), the second (9%) with only insignificant (plus or minus one year) differences between their

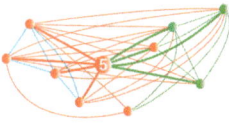

psychological and chronological age, and the third (55%), with a low psychological age ("younger"). In other words, most saw their future as far more dense than their past.

Conversations with the students revealed that their pending graduation compelled many to reconsider their life plans and reduce their aspirations. Some were, at "age seventeen, a youthful old man"[89] – already disappointed in the future, though not yet able to touch it.

Choosing a Profession and Students' Psychological Age

The task of choosing a profession is not tackled alone by an individual student. A vital influence is often exerted by close relatives, friends, and "other significant people," as well as the media. How does this influence the psychological age of an individual?

Both a sizeable and critical influence comes from the father (the value of the future is magnified and the student "seems younger"). Another powerful influence comes from newspapers, radio, and television (the value of the past is magnified and makes students "more mature" or "older"). As a whole, the closer the direct, personal contact with the source of influence, the stronger the "rejuvenation potential."

However, does it change anything with regard to choice of profession whether students feel younger than their actual age? They reported three other variables as significant in their decision: the responsibility that comes with the goals and tasks that society places on those with a particular profession, the type of personality that characterizes people in a profession, and the principles or norms of people in a particular profession. We found that students who feel "younger" focused more on the "goals and problems of society," while those who felt "older" were more likely to focus on a "good position in society."

Still More about Psychological Age

Creativity and a distant perspective are possible at any age. Yet research shows a decrease in creative productivity and psycho-physiological functions after ages thirty or forty.[90] Note that these are only average results. Memory and intellect need not deteriorate in otherwise healthy individuals when they use and exercise it. Many active elderly scholars surpass their younger colleagues in tests of scientific content.

A recent 2016 research, *The Demographics of Innovation in the United States*, suggests that many inventors don't peak until late in their careers, like 94 year-old John Goudenough, who made headlines in 2017 when he led a team that achieved a big breakthrough: a low-cost, all solid-state battery that could power the next generation of electric cars (*AARP Bulletin*, May 2017).

The secret to a creative attitude toward life is simple. For every year, for the rest of your life, despite how many years remain, surpass the previous year in what you achieve and experience. You will then maintain your psychological youth.

Wishes for Myself and Others:
The Psychology of Self-Improvement

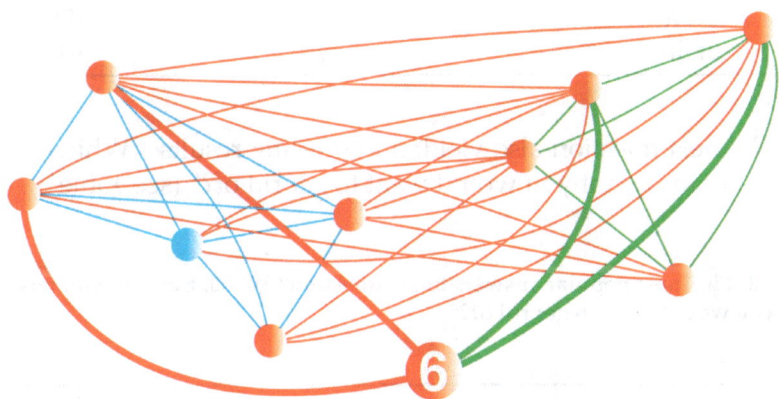

In each of us, as in a garden "with a hundred kinds of trees, a thousand kinds of flowers, a hundred kinds of fruit and vegetables,"[91] there resides, and clashes many different "selves" – a "past self," a "future self," a "real self," a "desired self," a "perceived self," a "self in the eyes of others," and many more. What would you like to become?

For a moment, forget what interferes with moving in the direction you desire. If, at this moment, you could change something about yourself, what would it be? With this question, a dialogue began with participants of our research on the problems of self-improvement and self-perceptions.[92]

What We Do Not Have

We asked fifty participants to name several personal qualities they felt that they were lacking (see Table 2).

Table 2. The most popular answers to the question "What qualities do you feel are missing in yourself?"

Confidence, decisiveness	46%
Endurance, composure	30%
Motivation, will power	30%
Tolerance	12%
Geniality	10%

The next question also yielded interesting results: "Which traits do you possess that you would want to get rid of?" (see Table 3).

Table 3. The most popular answers to the question "Which traits do you possess that you would want to get rid of?"

Disorganization	30%
Imbalance	28%
Uncertainty, indecisiveness	20%
Straightforwardness	16%
Laziness	16%

Nearly half the people lacked sufficient confidence; "solid materials" such as endurance, will power, and organization were needed. As for "soft components" (tolerance and geniality), only one in ten people found these qualities necessary. In a later question, the participants agreed to strike a deal with Mephistopheles, to give up an average of three years of their lives in exchange for the desirable qualities (the authors haggled in place of the devil).

In a follow-up question (see Table 4), we asked them, "Imagine you have the ability to change something in the psychology of another person. What would it be?"

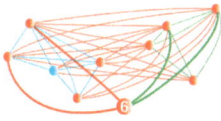

Table 4. The most popular answers to the question "Imagine you have the ability to change something in the psychology of another person, what would it be?"

Kindness, humanity	50%
Honesty, decency	30%
Mutual understanding, sympathy	22%
Tolerance	16%
Altruism, generosity	12%

It seems that the material with which we would like to build others is much softer than that which we would use on ourselves. A similar picture is apparent in response to the last question (see Table 5): "Which quality would you want to remove from other people?"

Table 5. The most popular answers to the question "Which traits would you want to remove from other people?"

Selfishness	28%
Dishonesty, indecency	26%
Viciousness, aggessiveness	22%
Narrowness, foolishness	18%
Envy	14%
Pragmatism	14%
Greed	14%

To achieve this last goal, the research participants were willing to give up six full years of their own lives to Mephistopheles. They felt such a shortage of kindness and decency in others that they were prepared to trade twice as much time of their lives to improve those around them rather than to attain personal perfection.

So, what is a psychologist to do? Fortify a person's character with confidence, endurance, will power, and other sound qualities that people wish to have, or soften a person's disposition with kindness, restraining any feeling of haughtiness, as others wish? And who are these other people that are not kind, decent, or responsive enough? Unfortunately, we are these people ourselves – in the eyes of others. We see in others what we do not see in ourselves.

The data indicate that a shortage of kindness in ourselves is noticed five times less frequently than in others. Were we lucky, and was it pure coincidence that the fifty participants (from Moscow and Kiev) were primarily kind in nature but, at some point, wounded by hurtful people? The probability of this occurring is slim.

Still, to verify our conclusions, we conducted a new, group experiment with forty participants in the city of Kerch on the Crimean seacoast. We asked, "What quality would you like to add to yourself?" Sample responses were to be calm, to have a sense of humor, determination, endurance, confidence, and will power.

One of the authors expressed his desire to become softer. But the participants' wishes continued along the same lines, that is, to be stronger. After the next ten responses, the second author suggested "benevolence to other people?" Yet, even with prompting, the participants did not change the general direction of their responses. Only one wanted more sympathy and understanding for others, and three wished for a sense of humor.

When we asked, "What quality would you like other people to add?", we found common ground again in terms of kindness, sympathy, thoughtfulness, and understanding. One person also wished everyone good health. These responses were consistent in both group and individual interviews.

The Insidious Rule of Psychological Improvement

Only four people noticed a shortage of softness in themselves, but did so equally as they looked at others. This type of person seemed to want to be more benevolent in a world that would, in turn, be kind back to them. Four other people wanted to become tougher among others.

We concluded that a "rule of psychological improvement" (ourselves – toughness; others – softness) existed to guide the desired self. However, we noted exceptions in some people who wished for reciprocal softness and reciprocal toughness.

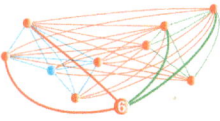

The Role of the Psychologist

A psychologist can help people psychologically improve, but whether or not they seek such assistance remains a major factor in their success. We asked, "How many hours each week and during what designated period are you ready to work on yourself with experienced psychologists to help you move in the desired direction?" Only four people completely rejected a psychologist's assistance, preferring to rely solely on personal strength and not reveal a "weak" side. While understandable, it is not wise to "white wash your inherent faults with your acquired virtues," as Kahil Gibran advises; instead, owning the bad with the good, as he says, "I would have the faults, they are like mine own."[93]

Still, most of the participants were consistent in their desire to change themselves, willing to spend two hours a day for one year (nearly 600 hours), working with a psychologist to ensure that at least one quality of their "desired self" became real. We have found, though, that even small amounts of time (30 to 90 hours) of group classes in psychological training for sociability, endurance, decisiveness and understanding others' intentions would suffice.

So time is available both for psychologists and the public to satisfy many people's need for self-improvement. However, once the skills of toughness are developed, people can slip easily into an inferiority complex, just a short step away.

Others expect kindness, understanding, and decency from you. However, we move away from their expectations. As a result, mutual dissatisfaction and tension increase, and a feeling of inferiority can further develop, leading to the desire to become even stronger.

Our decisiveness, often achieved through suffering, will not necessarily help others to become softer, nor will our strength necessarily make others love and understand us. Since a person's nature is not always generous, we found the most success in following the rules of psychological culture: wish for yourself what you would wish for others. In other words, if you feel a lack of kindness from others, then be kinder. If you are not understood, try first to understand others. If you sense a lack of honesty around you, become more honest yourself.

This conclusion is both perfectly logical yet paradoxical: a man, for example, wants one thing for himself, while a psychologist is able to offer him something else. In a store, if a customer asked for shoes but was offered a hat, this matter would end in a complaint. But in a psychologist's office, be prepared for such a paradox.

A Test for You

Almost everyone would like to see themselves and others as perfect, though we all lack a number of strengths in terms of character. If you could improve only one of the following characteristics – Endurance, Kindness, Sincerity, Willpower, Sympathy, or Confidence – in yourself, and only one in other people, which would be those two qualities?

Table 6. Test for you: Change yourself and others.

Yourself		Others					
		1	2	3	4	5	6
Endurance	1	A	B	B	A	B	A
Kindness	2	C	D	D	C	D	C
Sincerity	3	C	D	D	C	D	C
Will Power	4	A	B	B	A	B	A
Sympathy	5	C	D	D	C	D	C
Confidence	6	A	B	B	A	B	A

In Table 6, note the four types of psychological self-improvement we identified. Yours can be found by looking at the intersection of the horizontal and vertical axes, and finding the corresponding letter.

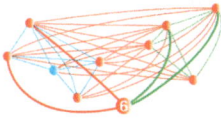

In summary,

"As" become tougher along with others (to make the world stronger),

"Bs" gain a foothold in a soft environment,

"Cs" soften their personality to help others gain a foothold, and

"Ds" become softer along with others (to make the world kinder).

And where are you today?

What to Expect in Talks with LifeLook®

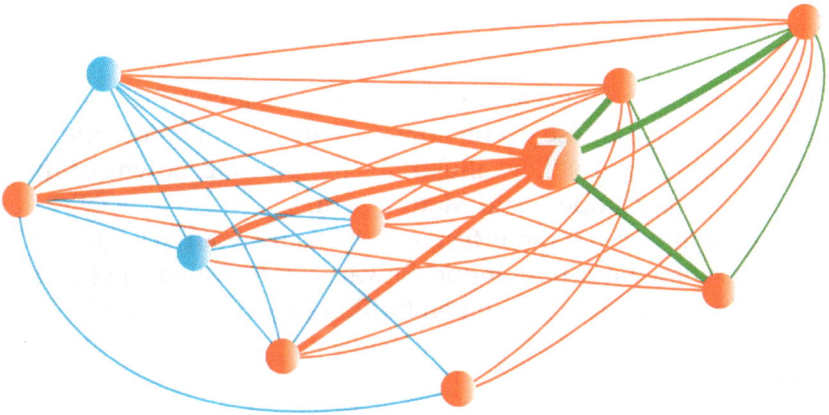

At least twice a year – at New Year's and birthdays – many people look back upon their lives and may even, in a way, have the feeling they can start their lives anew. The computer program we developed, LifeLook can help you better understand yourself and your past and to better map out your new life.[94]

Ancient Babylonians consulted the *Book of Fortunes*[95] while Chinese sages wrote the *Book of Change.*[96] Many people read the meaning of birds flying or the position of stars against the dome of the night sky, chips burning, or intricate patterns on their own palms. Since time immemorial, humanity has been looking for a means to reveal and create order in the kaleidoscope of life events, affairs and concerns.

LifeLook can help you self-analyze, such as when you give yourself to meditation on the eternal subject of transient human life; it is a means to help you get your bearings on your lifemap. LifeLook will ask questions, propose game tasks and investigate answers attentively before it expresses its opinion of you.

As you are to go through nine, biographic, self-analysis procedures (in Five-Year Periods, Events, Dates, Spheres, Colors, Goals,

Minutes, Causes, and Significances), you will be able to make an imaginary trip over your life map to more precisely determine the role of each event, to look at your psychological portrait and even introduce some corrections to it.

Five-Year Periods

You will evaluate different periods based on their eventfulness and the importance of these events to you. A mountain landscape with peaks, canyons and valleys illustrates the ups and downs of these events. "Life is a slope," said Maupassant.[97]

This simple biographic test will measure your psychological age, as discussed in Chapter one. Beware while evaluating the five-year periods. Don't be lazy when thinking about the future!

Events and Dates

Fancy you are creating a film about yourself and need to identify the main frames (events) of your past, present and future (yes, future, too!).

Events may be any changes in your inner and outer world, such as natural cataclysms and political restructurings, personal flights and falls, loves and disappointments, meetings and partings, diseases, sport achievements, travels, successes and failures of friends, children or relatives, among other things. Any change in life is an event that occurs quickly enough so that it is possible to indicate its date. There are also long stages in life, but for LifeLook, an "event" will be either the start or the end. For example, you would not list "education at a college" (a rather long stage), but rather, "entering a college" or "graduation."

Now briefly list 15-21 events on the screen cards. The more you input, the more reliable are the conclusions of LifeLook. When the event has already occurred, write when it happened. If it is a future event, indicate its approximate date. Calculations and experiments show that fewer than 15 events are not enough to build a full picture of your lifespan. On the other hand, the number of significant events in one's life is limited, and their composition changes over time. Things that seem important now may carry less weight later

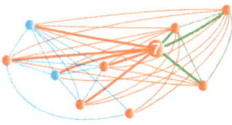

on, but 21 events can remain most important for several years. Other events that may seem less importnt may give place in the soul to other new events, feelings and plans.

It is interesting that medieval icon painters seem to have known it without any calculations. When depicting the life of a saint, they restricted themselves in most cases to fifteen or twenty episodes from his or her holy life. The LifeLook program follows the example of the old masters. Although we are not saints, each one of us can succeed in finding 21 significant life events.

Spheres

LifeLook respects personal secrets and does not demand excessive frankness. Place your events within the seven spheres: nature, society, job, family, inner world, health and spare time. An event may be simultaneously referred to several spheres, but specify the main one. The program now forms a preliminary opinion of you and organizes the subsequent dialogue more economically.

Colors

From the onscreen palette, select the color you associate with the event. The "film" LifeLook illustrates your life, identifies your attitude toward the events, and reports it later.

Goals

A goal is something you wish (or wished) to achieve, to bring closer in time or to postpone by undertaking an action (event). Goals and results do not always coincide. For example, if you go to a shop to buy a box of candy and suddenly run into a good friend, your goal was to buy candy, not to meet a friend. On the screen, the situation would look somewhat like Figure 4.

I Went Shopping		I Went Shopping
> definitely to achieve		definitely to achieve
probably to achieve		probably to achieve
possibly to achieve		possibly to achieve
independent of	>	independent of
possibly to avoid		possibly to avoid
probably to avoid		probably to avoid
definitely to avoid		definitely to avoid
I Bought Candy		**I Met My Friend**

Figure 4. Options in the procedure of goal-instrumental analysis.

The cursor (>) denotes the presence of an objective connection in the first case and the lack of such in the second. True, some people happen to go shopping for the opportunity to make an acquaintance. In this case, you would have to select one of the lines containing the word "achieve."

So think of your goals attentively. Different pairs of events will appear on the screen, and you will have to determine if one is a goal of the other. Some events may happen to have no goals (not everything occurs for a purpose). There happens, however, to be subconscious, half forgotten goals, which, for some reason, you would not like to speak about, even to yourself. You will have a chance to take a more mature look at your life.

The program offers a short and a full procedure of goal analysis. In the short variant, you only need to analyze the most probable goal related pairs of events given by LifeLook. The program sorts them out judging by their relative significance (the order of card creation and evaluation of five-year periods), spheres, and dates. Once the short procedure is completed, you may start the full goal analysis. You will only need time and patience, as the number of possible combinations can be impressive, especially if you made more than 15 event cards.

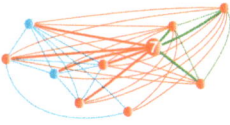

Minutes

LifeLook also offers an exercise in time estimation. This is not only interesting but useful as a moment of relaxation while staying connected to the program.

Causes

Goals are already known, but the plot of your life "film" is not yet clear. Why have events occurred? What enabled them and what hindered them? The goal of an event is always ahead of it in the future; the cause is always behind in the past. It is difficult to list all the causes even for one event, but some may appear on your list.

As before, different pairs of events will appear on the screen. You will unravel the threads of causes and consequences by selecting the most true statement on the nature of their connection. Take, for example, the pairing, as seen in Figure 5.

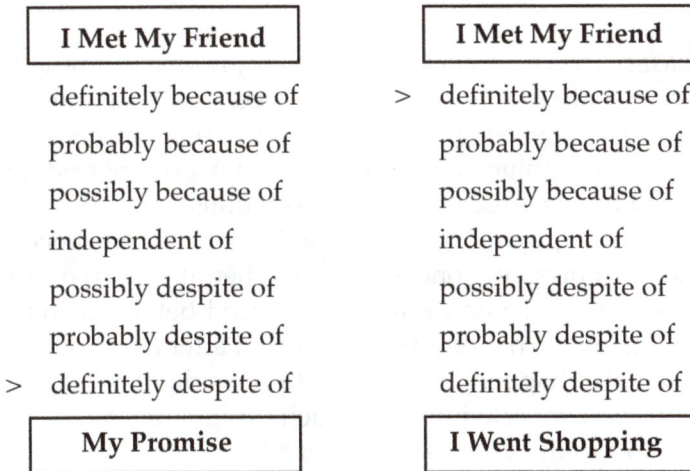

I Met My Friend		**I Met My Friend**
definitely because of	>	definitely because of
probably because of		probably because of
possibly because of		possibly because of
independent of		independent of
possibly despite of		possibly despite of
probably despite of		probably despite of
> definitely despite of		definitely despite of
My Promise		**I Went Shopping**

Figure 5. Options in the procedure of cause-and-effect analysis.

The relationships are obvious here if you promised not to see that friend anymore. But it may be more complicated when you shuffle the events of your real life. When you feel one of them is a help or a hindrance to another, indicate this, regardless of whether some more evident and immediate causes are available.

Significances

Now, at last, you will be able to know the value (significance) of each event. As you evaluate events by significance, LifeLook will assess how realistic your evaluations are, and why you sometimes make mistakes. To get the actual value of a particular event, LifeLook has calculated the number of its causal and goal connections. Psychological studies have shown that the number of interconnections with other events reflects how intimately they are intertwined with life. In everyday life, it may be difficult to realize all the existing connections; some are non-actual, others undesirable, and some too weak to warrant our attention. Different psychological barriers and defenses often lead to peculiar illusions: we make a mountain out of a molehill or consider significant events to be trifle. If you want a sober look at reality, devoid of illusion, see what you get in a LifeLook chart.

LifeMap

The LifeMap drawn by LifeLook is a graphic representation of events and their interconnections (see, for example, Figure 3, page 16). By their colors you can see the relation between the psychological past (blue lines of recollections), present (red lines of feelings) and future (green lines of expectations).

LifeMap is a graph. The vertical axis is the significance of an event, and the horizontal one is the age when it occurred or is expected to occur. When an event has occurred before the birthday date (these things do happen!) or is expected after the supposed life span (as can also happen), it lies a bit to the side of the horizontal axis. Events are connected by lines, each designating a connection: to achieve, to avoid, thanks to, despite.

LifeMap shows the plot of your life. Interacting with LifeLook, you were the hero of the imaginary film and its scriptwriter. Now the script is finished, and it is time to see the episodes of the film (i.e. to make a trip from the "long ago" to the "not too soon"). You will learn the morning of your life, the afternoon, and when the night will fall. Be prepared for surprises: the clock of your life and the calendar do not always coincide.

Psychological Portrait

At the end of your LifeLook, you will get a description of your personal characteristics and psychological age. It will also reveal the scale of your intentions, attitudes toward life difficulties, sense of reality, emotional sensitivity, satisfaction with life, desire and ability to plan life. It assesses your self-confidence, defines your general type and lifestyle. It will also tell you what has changed in your character recently and what is about to change in the near future.

These final descriptions are based on many indexes (see Table 11, page 99, and Appendix) and offer the possibility of psychological autocorrection after you have familiarized yourself with the LifeLook portrait. Of course, self-perfection is only justified after an honest self-analysis, just as it is better to smooth your hair while looking at yourself in the mirror.

Implementation and Age

The first characteristic shown in the portrait is the implementation of your life intentions, on a scale of 0 to 100 percent. The last is psychological age (as discussed earlier). When the implementation and age seem to be too high, we suggest you revise your evaluations of the five-year periods to find bolder prospects, or evaluate your past more moderately. In any case, you will get a chance to become younger. Those who wish to become more mature will, however, have to extract a more valuable experience from the past; if this fails, you can only moderate your dreams. Age correction will remain only a curious psychological game if you don't modify your evaluations by adding new, important events to the future (when wishing to become younger) or to the past (when wishing to become more mature). At least go to the program's "information on events," to write down new events, dates, spheres, and colors. If you reanalyze the goals and causes of your new events, then LifeMap will change and your psychological age will essentially change with it.

Strategic Thinking

LifeLook can also "read between the lines" on implementation and age. First, it will determine whether you are a strategist, a tactician, or a person preoccupied with the current situation. The concept is based on the life intentions scale, which is proportional to the length of time for the goals, causes and sequences you are able to trace down, and your confidence in revealing interdependence between different LifeLook events.

Each of the types, i.e. a strategist, a tactician and a situationist, has benefits and disadvantages. At the same time, research studies show that people with large-scale intentions have a more responsible attitude toward the past and the future, find their vocation more quickly and more accurately. Therefore, look for a fulcrum in a more distant past or future when life seems to lose its sense for you. Go to the program's "information on events," to replace less significant events through deeper recollections and more distant expectations. Turn to the "causes" and "goals" procedures, then look for your new sources and prospects more confidently. You will find that not all the fruits of your glorious deeds have ripened yet; there is energy and audacity to begin a project that may take more than a lifetime to realize (And if one life turns out to be enough? A strategist has more than one life, you know). After that, follow Hans Selye's rule:

> Fight for your highest attainable aim
> But never put up resistance in vain.[98]

Difficulties

LifeLook recognizes your problems signaled by the words "despite" and "avoid" you used in analyzing causes and goals. The number of negative connections in the total sum states how easy or difficult your life actually is.

If you feel an excess of difficulties, try to train yourself at least not to focus on them. A return to the "goals" and "causes" procedures may help you. Try to use the words "possibly, despite" or "possibly, avoid" instead of "definitely/probably, despite," "defi-

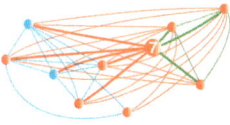

nitely/probably, avoid," where it doesn't essentially change the sense of your answers.

Sometimes it is worth accepting the "unavoidable at all" choice, and note the independence of events that appeared to hinder each other. There is always another way to withstand difficulties: maybe, if you are not using all available resources, you may notice new means to achieve your goals and new favorable conditions. It may be better to say "probably" or even "definitely" instead of "possibly to achieve," with more confidence. If this training helps you modify the respective traits on your portrait, you may also succeed in making your real life easier.

Sense of Reality

The following fragment of the portrait characterizes your sense of reality in evaluating the significance of events. Your evaluations may either be close to the real status of events, independent of it, or even contradict it. Personal characteristics, such as independence, conformity and acceptance of reality, can show a powerful psychological defense corresponding to these variants. Improve your sense of reality by going through the "significances" procedure once more. The developers of the program nicknamed this procedure "sage," since it teaches you to be real in evaluating achievements and failures.

Emotions and Satisfaction

LifeLook's conclusions about emotional sensitivity, optimism and pessimism are drawn on the basis of color preferences for different events. If you prefer to see events in extreme colors (very pleasant or very unpleasant for you), LifeLook will note that you are rather emotional. Your optimism depends on how often you color events in pleasant colors. The same idea is behind conclusions about your emotional attitude to different events. Pay attention to the opinion of LifeLook, as it reflects feelings you are sometimes not aware of having. As a result of a successful biographic self-analysis, these feelings often become more clear, so go back to re-color everything, as if for the first time. Even without changing events, you may find more bright feelings and satisfaction with life.

Desire and Ability to Plan. Confidence

Your desire and ability to plan life may become easier when you compare the results of the goals and causes analyses. Your persistence is reflected in the words "achieve" and "avoid." If your friends say you are too practical, we recommend you try to mention the words "achieve" and "avoid" less often in your next talk with LifeLook, or to soothe them (by using the terms "probably" and "possibly" instead of "definitely" where it doesn't infringe on your principles). However, if you notice that you are "going with the flow," look again for goals in the available events.

Mistakes can occur in any plan; for example, sports exercises for preventing injury may also cause serious injuries. To reveal such mistakes, LifeLook compares goals and means with consequences and causes of different events, then assesses whether you are selecting the best means for achieving your life goals. Surely, to err is human. But when there are too many mistakes, it may be worth changing your thinking by revisiting the "causes" and "goals" section of this program.

The more categorical you are in these statements, considering events to be "definitely" connected or not, the more confident you look in your portrait. To be tolerant of "probably" and "possibly" means to become softer, less categorical.

Types of Humans

We are all *Homo sapiens* (*Hominis sapientis*).[99] LifeLook respects this science, but also those thinkers who gave Man (i.e. humanity including both men and women) such epithets as *Homo politicus, Homo faber, Homo ludens, Homo patient, Homo liber,* etc. Following this tradition, the LifeLook program uses the typology: *public-oriented, nature-oriented, family-oriented, work-oriented, inwardly-oriented, health-oriented, and leisure-oriented person.* Your type depends on what spheres are most filled with significant events and connections. People of one type live as if in the same world, home, and life space. But their lifestyles may differ as each has a unique path to happiness.

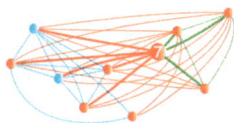

LifeLook describes lifestyle, for example, as either contemplative/active or ascetic/hedonistic. There is a number of principal styles, determined by correlating connections between events. Each connection (achieve, avoid, because, despite) shows the person's self-restraint or self-development, a cognition about the world or using it. Ancient philosophers originally offered these paths to happiness.

Your Type and Style are fundamental psychological characteristics difficult to change without betraying yourself and, therefore, you need no correction in the LifeLook program. If someone does not like your fundamental characteristics, consider distancing yourself from that person rather than damaging your personality.

Dynamics and Forecast

Your general characteristics will be supplemented by conclusions about features that can change. LifeLook compares and analyzes the distinguishing features of three moments in your life—the current moment, the nearest past and the nearest future—to tell you how your character has changed since the last event, and how it may change after the next one.

Additional Opportunities

The main purpose of LifeLook is to help you in the psychological analysis of your private life though it may also be of use in analyzing the life lines of other people. It is an interesting, but not a simple task to comprehend the life of a husband or wife, for example, or children, friends, parents, and political figures. To do so requires transforming yourself mentally into another person, and having a talk with LifeLook as if you were someone else. You may make many discoveries, although you will see how incomplete your notions are of even the closest people to you. Such an experience will, at least, make you more attentive to them.

The program may also assist teachers, historians, reporters, lawyers, and writers to delve into a person's life story and understand his or her motivations more clearly. We hope that, besides satisfying a person's casual curiosity or the professional interest of a specialist, LifeLook will meet the creative demands of a playwright, a producer, or an actor who has to invent and play the lives of characters. For example, Peter Stormare, a Swedish actor who played Hamlet at the Royal Dramatic Theater, directed by Ingmar Bergman, used LifeLook to analyze Hamlet's life. Our initial goal was to understand the psychological background against which the father's death touched Hamlet. Stormare was asked to recreate Hamlet's inner life and intentions at least a month before the tragic events began. At this time, the King is alive and the Prince continues his usual lifestyle.

In Bergman and Stormare's interpretation, Hamlet did not live in Shakespearean times at all. According to the actor, he was born in October, 1881, and is now thirty, so the year is 1911. Stormare's Hamlet meditates on his past and future, finds the 15 most important events, determines their causes and goals; in a word, he works with LifeLook.

The actor, as Hamlet, sees his life as follows: he became aware of the gift of God, one of the two most valuable events, at the age of 11, half a year before his sister died. At age 17, Hamlet fell in love for the first time, and at age 20, he left home with bad feelings. In May, 1908, at the age of 26, Hamlet wrote his first book and in July got married. Hamlet is now thirty. What does he expect?

The picture of the near future is rather gloomy: his father's death within a year, divorce in 2 years, and war in 4 years. After that murky period, by age 34, Hamlet hopes to meet the mother of his future son. At 37, he will be glad to devote himself to creative work in literature and, at 42, he intends to become a member of the Academy. To all appearances, it is the peak of his creativity; after that, his mother's diseased eyes and death loom ahead.

Such are Hamlet's intentions and the state of his spirit on the verge of tragic changes. With LifeLook, you too can play any role and better understand both fictional characters and people about whom you care.

Time-Oriented Psychotherapy for Chernobyl Disaster–Affected Children

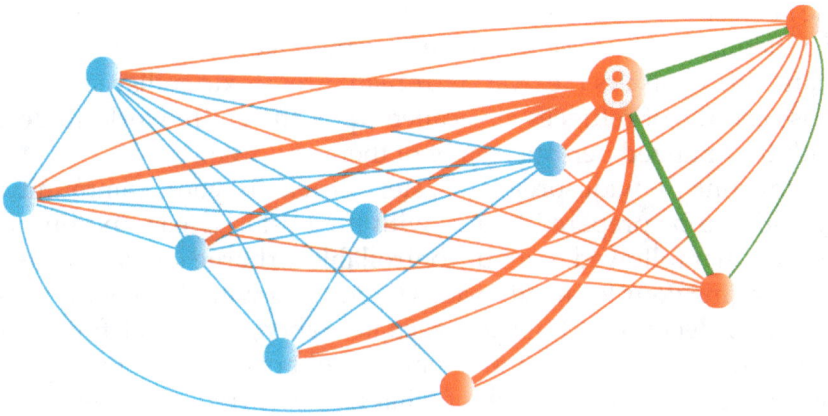

The remarkable thing about LifeLook is also its ability to assist psychologists in addressing post-traumatic responses, such as in Chernobyl disaster-affected children. Mental health professionals who worked with this population after the 1986 disaster, reported that the children experienced distorted thoughts and feelings about their past, present and future much more than other children their age.

The people, who were young at the time of the Chernobyl explosion, realized they could never return home. They knew that illnesses may befall them, their parents may die sooner than normal, and their environment was poisoned. The psychotherapeutic software program provided psychological support in a school setting to 41 of the evacuated adolescents who continued to experience aftereffects of the Chernobyl explosion.[100] In this clinical research, we used the program called *LifeLine*[101], the original Russian-language version of LifeLook. The current name, LifeLook, is used instead in this book.

Background

Experiences of trauma and disaster are well known for their potential to shatter world assumptions,[102] darken expectations, and create the sense of a foreshortened future, especially in children. Each year, entire communities in the United States and abroad face the necessity of addressing children's responses to natural disasters (i.e. floods, hurricanes, tornadoes, earthquakes, etc.) as well as in manmade disasters (i.e. war, terrorism, fires, toxic spills, etc.). The mass exodus of refugees also called upon the entire world to deal with traumatized persons, many of them children.

Imagine if widespread disaster struck in your community. Would you be prepared to deal with the hysteria, fear, and uncertainties that followed, with uncontrollable airborne contaminants?

Imagine your local authorities interacting with the federal government, deciding whom to evacuate, when, how and for what duration of time, as you and your neighbors wait, both hoping and fearing to hear the truth of what had occurred. Imagine learning that your drinking water may be contaminated with invisible, tasteless radionuclides, that the air is unsafe to breathe, that even walking outdoors may be dangerous. Then imagine a disaster with effects that last for decades, even centuries later, poisoning the soil, the vegetation, the animals, the food and the homes of an entire region.

The Chernobyl Explosion

Chernobyl is perhaps the largest disaster ever caused by humans. In the Spring of 1986, a plume of volatile radioactive elements exploded into the atmosphere, which have been estimated to be between 10 to 90 times the amount released at Hiroshima.[103] Later, the explosion was found to be the result of an error in routine testing which resulted in radioactive fallout blanketing a third of Belarus, as well as contaminating northern Ukraine and parts of Russia.

More than 17 million people, of whom 2.5 million were children below the age of 5, suffered some degree of radioactive contamination.[104] Thousands were evacuated from their homes with very

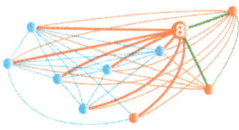

short notice, being told to take nothing with them, as all was contaminated. Hundreds of communities were declared uninhabitable.

Crews of over 600,000 military, police and fire-fighters (later referred to as "liquidators") were sent in to fight the nuclear fire and to close off the radioactive leakage. Many of these heroes later became gravely ill and died, some on the spot, from radiation poisoning. Many of these same workers were also sent in to bulldoze evacuated communities, shoot all the contaminated livestock and pets, and bury forever the contaminated homes and buildings of the communities they destroyed. An uninhabitable radioactive zone was declared surrounding the nuclear plant, and fences were erected to keep inhabitants from ever returning to what had been their homes and farmlands.

Over time, researchers and scientists descended upon this nightmare zone to study the effects of the disaster. Maps were drawn showing the lands where most of the contamination fell. Even more evacuations and relocations occurred, but sadly, the extent of damage was so great that some people would have no choice but to continue living where contamination had fallen.

Foretelling effects of the disaster twenty years before Chernobyl, one of the first radiation psychologists explained that "Power plants will create more and cheaper energy sources; but power plants will create health hazards and contamination."[105]

Worse, immediately after the Chernobyl disaster, the public was not told of the danger. Many, especially those living in Belarus, were not given the entire truth even when they were told. As a result, many children received high doses of radiation and many ingested highly radioactive foods. The most striking health consequences has been a 300-fold increase in thyroid cancer among children in the affected areas.[106] Adolescents in the region undergo yearly thyroid examinations, and those affected have surgery to remove the malignant portion of their thyroid gland.

Hysteria and distrust in government continues. The population lives in fear that leukemia, blood disorders and a whole array of psychosomatic symptoms may result from the radioactive contamination. Researchers found evidence of preoccupation with radiation fears and mental and bodily distress as the result of worries over the safety of food and environment, even a decade after the explosion.[107] In Belarus, where the majority of radiation fell, the situation was especially grim, with children often identified as having high doses of total body radionuclides from contaminated foods and milk,[108] including those born well after the disaster.

To deal with the pervasive fear of an environmental toxin is a very difficult task particularly when the fears are based, at least still partially, in reality, even years after the event.[109]

The issues at stake include: (a) fears of the unknown; (b) issues of distrust in authorities and sources of information pertaining to the toxin; (c) anxieties over issues of preventing contamination or already having become contaminated; (d) stigma for those who know they have been contaminated (i.e. in this disaster being labeled as a "Chernobyl" which is what evacuees are often called, or having a "Chernobyl necklace," which is a scar across the neck that bears grim witness to the removal of the affected thyroid); and (e) fears of what contamination may bring in terms of adverse health consequences in the future.[110]

The Chernobyl explosion also became an "organizing event" for millions of people who viewed life before and after the disaster as almost two separate lifetimes. It is not insignificant to note that during the time leading up to and following Chernobyl, the collapse of the former Soviet Union was imminent. Therefore, it was not only a nuclear disaster and its fallout that disrupted lives, but the stress of the unknown in the final months of the Soviet Union. However, our research was conducted before the political collapse, so the major disrupter at that time was still Chernobyl.

The day after the Chernobyl explosion, all 49,000 residents of Pripyat, a town located 4 km (2.5 miles) from the nuclear power reactor, including workers and their families, were evacuated. These individuals experienced triple stressors from the explosion: radioactivity before evacuation, the evacuation itself, and subsequent relocation.[111] Many children were temporarily separated from their parents, and many pregnant women were encouraged to accept government-recommended abortions. The effects on children exposed to the Chernobyl situation were especially traumatic.[112]

Intervention for Chernobyl Evacuee Children

We went to a school in Kiev, Ukraine, in October and November 1991, to evaluate forty-one of the Pripyat-evacuated children who did not display obvious ill health. At the time of the explosion, the children were between 7 and 11 years of age; our research took place five years later. We had two goals: to analyze how these children viewed the probable course of their lives and to test our new computer-assisted techniques for psychological support in traumatic situations, developed shortly before the accident.[113]

LifeLook for Trauma Victims

The primary concept of the goal-and-causal theory of psychological time[114] is that human experiences of time, place, continuity, sense of age, etc. depend on the way significant life events are perceived to be connected. Traumatic events often remain in the psychological present much longer than normal events. As a result, any unresolved traumatic experiences can overshadow all other events.

Traumatized individuals frequently report that their experience has caused them to become disconnected from others, from the rest of life and, particularly, from optimistic views of the future. It is also commonly reported that unresolved traumas may distort time and be experienced by the sufferer as intrusively present, despite the passage of time. The LifeLook program has a remediative function in this regard, in that it offers new ways of perceiving how time (personal past, present and future) may be experienced. LifeLook can also help to incorporate an overwhelmingly traumatic event into one's life narrative in a manner that makes it less of a dominating, overshadowing event. Instead, the event is brought into context with experiences that have gone before, and those yet to come, to help bring about a more positive life orientation.

During a one-to-two hour dialogue with the program, the 41 children were asked to follow the standard procedures outlined in Chapter 7 and summarized here: (a) to estimate the eventfulness of five-year periods; (b) to indicate up to 21 important life events in different domains[115] of his/her past, present, and future; (c) to estimate the date of the events; (d) to assign the appropriate emotional tone by selecting one (of eight) Lusher Color Test colors[116] they associated with the event; and (e) to think about various goals and causal relationships between the events. Each individual received a printout of his/her psychological characteristics and a LifeMap, a graphic display of all significant moments in his/her life in the coordinates of age and motivational status[117] (see, for example, Figure 6).

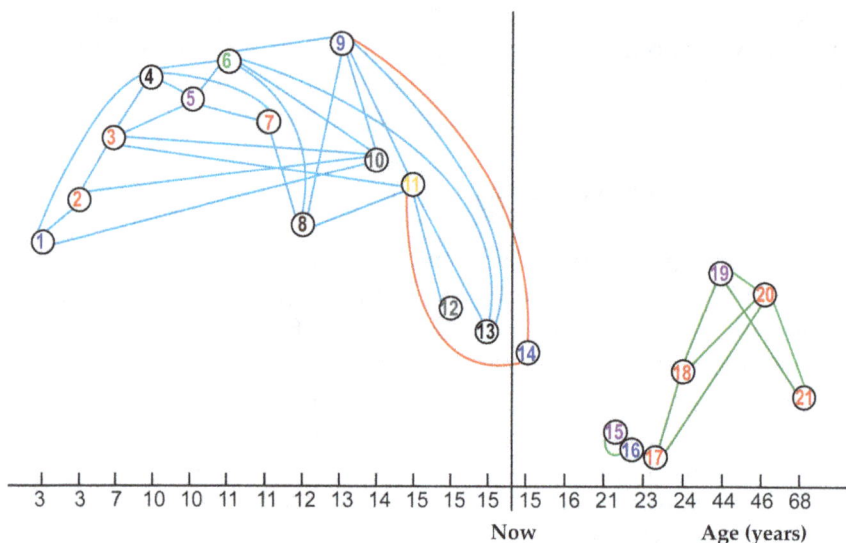

Figure 6. A life map showing feelings of a lack of prospects (Galina, age 15). List of life events: (1) kindergarten; (2) birth of brother; (3) pool; (4) disaster; (5) new school; (6) new life; (7) Kiev; (8) acquaintances; (9) relationships; (10) parents; (11) outstanding time; (12) boredom; (13) disenchantment; (14) brother; (15) starting university; (16) starting work; (17) marriage; (18) birth of child; (19) child's marriage; (20) a grandchild appears; (21) a great-grandchild appears.

With the LifeMap and printout, each child if he or she desired, could then make changes in the way he/she feels, perceives and behaves in certain areas.

Middle school and high school students are old enough to use all of the features of the LifeLook program. The psychologist's role was to (1) give some assistance during the client-computer dialogue, (2) provide analysis of the psychobiographical dates and findings from the therapeutic viewpoint, and (3) offer suggestions of alternative ways by which to view one's life, which might fa-

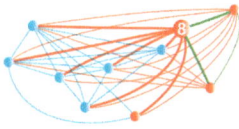

cilitate constructive changes in past memories, future expectations, and present experiences.

One advantage of LifeLook is to maximize limited resources during community-wide traumas and disasters so that a single psychologist would be able to interact on a meaningful level with many students, even in a limited amount of time. A single professional has at his or her disposal a powerful tool to assist many students in reorganizing their thinking or orientation to life, which may have turned negative as a result of the traumatic experience.

As expected, the children who experienced the Chernobyl disaster were found to have a distorted view of life.

The Dynamics of Coping with a Traumatic Event

To successfully move beyond a traumatic event, one must incorporate into one's mind what has been a terrifying, overwhelming and hurtful experience. Often the emotional and sensory aspects of the trauma are so overwhelming that the experience seems impossible to incorporate into existing schemas. When the mind is unable to process the experience, a posttraumatic decline is typical. The mind becomes "trauma-organized," creating a post-trauma history in which avoidance, intrusion and hyperarousal become dominant life themes. This is the typical pattern for post-traumatic stress disorders (PTSD).

Brain researchers studying PTSD report that such trauma-organized minds appear to be dominated by affective and sensory memories that, unlike normal memories, fire from the amygdala and hippocampal regions. Researchers and clinicians agree that reaching a trauma-resolved state would require moving traumatic memories from primary limbic memory systems to higher cortical systems of memory which involve cognition and language.[118]

Unprocessed limbic memories keep past traumas present by continually alerting the body to danger, despite the passage of time following the trauma. This bodily state of alarm, as well as the mind's attempts at defense, continues unabated until the limbic memories are processed into less affectively-charged cognitions that reside in cortical regions of the brain. As higher-functioning memories, they cannot be so easily reconstructed and re-experienced in the present with the full sensations and affect they had originally carried.

While this change in trauma memories can be implemented in a multitude of ways, one common path is to address the trauma directly, speaking about it as in a therapy setting, such that memories transfer from limbic to cortical memories. Through discussion, a remediative process occurs in which shattered assumptions are addressed.

Likewise, therapeutic discussion aids in the construction of schemas that build both thoughts and relationships capable of "holding" the negative affects (fear, guilt, despair, helplessness). These emotions, the person originally experienced, continue to be trapped in the limbic system, and are repeatedly re-experienced until the trauma is "processed." Fostering such discussions was formerly seen as the domain of the psychologist. However, use of the LifeLook program with the supervision of a mental health worker also has the capability of beginning this restorative process, thereby creating a situation in which the trauma recedes from being dominant and can be contextualized into a life, which is viewed as rich in past, present and future experiences.

Phases of Coping with a Trauma Using the LifeLook Program

Sixty-seven percent of the Pripyat-evacuated adolescents identified the Chernobyl accident and/or the evacuation as among their 15 most important life events. Based on their experience, we subsequently identified six phases of their coping with an ongoing traumatic event, particularly a trauma that continues to hold the potential for ongoing horrific consequences long after the core event has occurred (i.e. childhood cancer, illness or, untimely death as a result of exposure to a toxin, or future disability arising out of exposure). While many traumas hold the potential for adverse and uncertain outcomes that the victim must await, exposure to toxins is a particular exemplar of this category.

The six phases of coping (see Figure 7) are as follows: (a) Perception of the traumatic event as an isolated fact, (b) Expectation of possible adverse consequences, and a search for reasons (e.g. causes and meanings), (c) Awareness of already occurring negative conse-

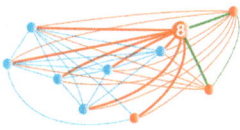

quences and a search for reasons, (d) A feeling that consequences of the traumatic event have all been exhausted and a search for reasons, (e) Devaluation of the consequences and loss of interest in a search for reasons, and (f) Devaluation of the fact of trauma.

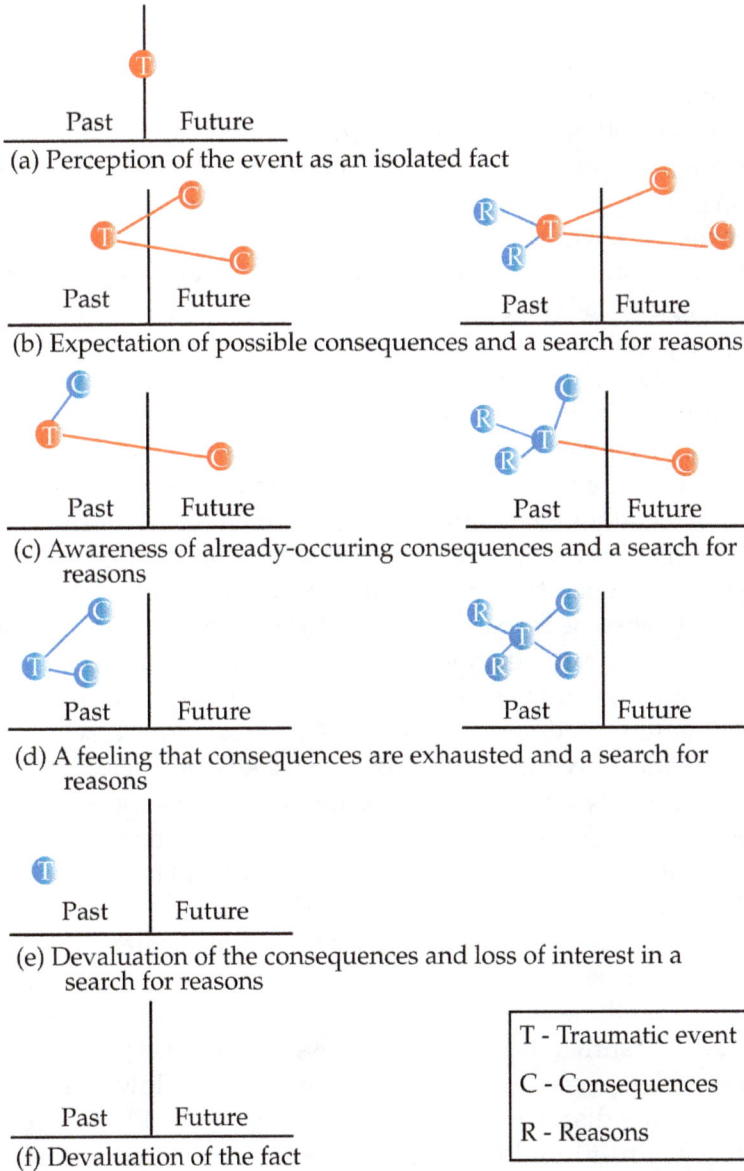

(a) Perception of the event as an isolated fact

(b) Expectation of possible consequences and a search for reasons

(c) Awareness of already-occuring consequences and a search for reasons

(d) A feeling that consequences are exhausted and a search for reasons

(e) Devaluation of the consequences and loss of interest in a search for reasons

(f) Devaluation of the fact

T - Traumatic event

C - Consequences

R - Reasons

Figure 7. Phases of coping with a traumatic event.

A very important aspect to understanding the individually-experienced trauma is to discover how a person views both the reasons (i.e. causes and meanings) and consequences of that trauma. In the first stage of coping, the trauma is perceived as an isolated fact not yet connected to other life events. This phase generally occurs in a state of anxious uncertainty as the mind struggles to incorporate the overwhelming aspects of the trauma into existing schemas, which are nevertheless unlikely to contain it. With exposure to toxins and other contaminating traumas (e.g. AIDS, poisoning) which have the potential for future and ongoing problems, the perception of how the trauma may connect to further consequences is more extended over time.

In the second phase, there is an awareness and expectation of the potential for adverse consequences. In Chernobyl evacuee children, this phase is associated with an expectation of disease and death (of oneself and/or loved ones). The disaster becomes the dominating event in the present. For children, this second phase is especially problematic, as it interferes with the normal orientation toward the future that is generally observed in adolescents.

Teens usually view themselves as invulnerable to normal danger, a defense mechanism which assists them in taking the frightening steps of separating from their parents to fulfill their potential as adults. (For some teens, this sense of invulnerability can become exaggerated and problematic, resulting in premature and extreme risk-taking behaviors with adverse results.) However, traumatized children entering adolescence are less able to adopt a schema of invulnerability, having been awakened to a keen awareness of their own vulnerability and the real potential for adverse personal consequences. The Chernobyl evacuees who saw a foreshortened future displayed no sense of invulnerability and had no zest to claim life, since their future had been poisoned.

In the second coping phase, the child is also caught between fear of future consequences of the trauma and the impossibility of seeing beyond these consequences. The gravity of a traumatic event can be significantly reduced if awareness of the consequences is accompanied by an active search for causes, which allows the victim to perceive the disaster in the context of the entire life course. As a person begins to understand the causes of a trauma, it loses its

acuteness and moves from the individual's psychological present to the psychological past. Likewise, viewing the trauma in the context of one's past actions and decision (versus only the present and future) makes it less acute. This concept is nearly always embedded in the traumatized person's questions of "Why did this happen to me?" Sometimes it is healing to understand one's personal responsibility as to why a trauma occurred, if indeed reasons exist, but other times, the answer may be as simple as "I happened to be in the way of catastrophe."

In either case, the trauma becomes less acute as the search for reasons is fulfilled. Understanding the reasons leading up to a trauma, whether unavoidable or triggered by one's actions, allows it to be accepted finally as an external fact which must be incorporated into life, with whatever it may now bring with it. Such an approach permits the victim to have a calmer and more sober attitude toward the event. It also helps an individual take protective actions in the present and future without being motivated only by the sheer terror of the unknown or by the belief that there will be no meaningful future. Contextualizing the trauma in life's narrative can also be a crucial aspect of releasing the speechless terror of trauma[119] to find its way into a more narrative, coherent memory process.

Figure 7b on page 69 illustrates this process for two high school seniors, Zhenya and Lena (all names have been changed), both former residents of Pripyat. Zhenya (Figure 7b left) connected the event only with the future: a trip to Germany and his own death. Lena (Figure 7b right) connected the disaster with her future as well, but she also connected it with the family's move from their small village to the town of Pripyat and her birth in the regional center before that. The emotional tone Lena assigned to the "disaster" event field was much calmer than was the case for Zhenya, as Lena's trauma had been contextualized into her life (past, present, and future) rather than seen as only dominating it in the present and future.

In the third phase of coping with trauma, a child sees that some consequences of the frightening event have already come to pass. The consequences may not be as terrible as he or she had feared; some are actually pleasant. In analyzing their lives in a dialogue with the computer, children who are in this phase, noted in calm and pleasant tones that, as a result of the disaster, they moved to the capital (Kiev), started to attend a new and bigger school, or were taken to the best summer camp, to the beach, and overseas.

The overall negative experiences arising from events connected with the disaster were significantly eased with some instances of positive emotions starting to dominate the traumatic event field. This commonly occurred with children from Pripyat, who become interested in science, physics and nuclear power engineering, and who entered, or prepared to enter, the corresponding university department. Some even felt themselves capable of making discoveries in this area.

The inner work of integrating the traumatic event into the context of the person's past continued throughout the third phase. Totally unexpected interpretations sometimes appeared at this point. Marina, born April 25 — the day before Chernobyl exploded — considered her birth to have been the second most important of her life (the expectation of giving birth to her own children in first place) and colored it red, her favorite color. She painted the disaster in her least favorite color, black, and put it in third place, but erroneously dated it the 25th of April (her birthday) instead of the date of the disaster — the 26th.

Which of these two polar experiences is the determining factor for the emotional coloring of her life as a whole, the darkness of disaster or the joy of having been born?

Due to the unexpected coincidence between the events, a synchronous connection can be easily established between the two. She indirectly asked, "Was I born for the disaster?" and answered, "Of course, in order to avoid it." She connected all of the events in her life with the disaster, but colored nearly all of them in the happy color of her birthday — red. These include starting school (age 8), closing of the nuclear power plant (12), going to the mountains (13), finishing school (16), wedding (18), children (age 20), apartment (21), children's wedding (39), going to Pripyat (70), anniversaries (16, 40, 50). Only receiving a pension at age 45 was given a neutral designation.

We can see that Marina's choice was uncompromising. She is an optimist. Her own birthday of April 25 and the optimistic pleasure of celebrating her entrance into life helps her to take on an orienta-

tion that protects her from the negative outlook that the trauma of April 26, 1986 could easily have painted. Orienting the trauma in the context of her birthday helps Marina to look past Chernobyl to a joyous event in the past, and beyond the disaster to all future joyous connecting birthdays. Every year on these dates, she is eager to rejoice about life and all else that may be taking place.

In the fourth coping phase, an individual comes to an understanding that the direct results of the traumatic event are finished, and life goes on. For the Chernobyl children, this phase was encountered by looking back at what had already occurred and projecting into their futures with the assistance of the LifeLook program. Although recollections of illnesses and losses were still encountered in the associated field of the accident and evacuation, these memories were fairly calm and also associated with bright recollections about moving to a new home, making new friends, and taking interesting trips. For the children who are viewing all of the consequences of a trauma as already finished, that trauma becomes fixed in the psychological past and has little power over the future.

By phase five, the traumatic event loses its dominance in life and is perceived as more of a local, isolated fact. Disaster consequences are devalued against the background of other, more important life events, while interest in finding causes for the former declines. As the trauma finds its place in an entire narrative of life in which the experience is but one of many events, former experiences associated with the trauma turn to recollections of something faintly unpleasant that happened in the distant past, versus strong affect overshadowing all else.

In the final phase of coping, devaluation of the fact occurs as well, the traumatic event having receded so far into the background that it is no longer even included in the list of meaningful events.

Various reactions to the traumatic event in these six phases also appear in children's estimation of their anticipated longevity. Strangely, the longest life estimations came from the second and most painful phase, when the disaster was still being experienced in a very significant and immediate manner. Anxiety about illness and death brings these events into the psychological present. In protecting the self against these anxieties, children often pushed estimates of longevity up to one hundred years or more.

These inflated self-estimates about longevity may be understood as a defense mechanism. They also reveal the possibility that the classic post-traumatic stress disorder literature referring to a sense of a foreshortened future may indicate only one of many potential trauma-related time- and age-distortions that can occur in children and adults.

In succeeding phases, as the intensity of the experience fades, life expectancies lowered to more realistic levels (for Ukraine, at that time), that is, 60-80 years. The realization of the consequences phase also had its share of pessimistic estimates. A background of actual illnesses and losses can shorten longevity estimates to 50 years. As a rule, these pessimistic estimations about longevity disappear in the devaluation of consequences phase. The hope of having a long life reappears.

Psychotherapeutic Techniques and Findings

Interviews with the 41 high school seniors evacuated from Pripyat the day after the Chernobyl disaster reveal the following distribution in their positions relative to coping phases of relating to the disaster (see Table 7).

Table 7. Number of Pripyat-evacuated children on different phases of coping with the traumatic event of the Chernobyl disaster (five years later).

Phases	Number of children N = 41
(a) Perception of the isolated fact	0
(b) Expectation of possible adverse consequences	6
(c) Awareness of already-occurring consequences	7
(d) A feeling that the consequences are exhausted	12
(e) Devaluation of the consequences	4
(f) Devaluation of the fact of trauma	12

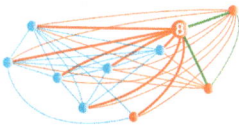

No children were in the first phase. We assumed that this was because five years had passed since the disaster, and they no longer viewed it as an isolated event unrelated to anything else. However, almost two thirds of them were in phases two through four, indicating that the disaster was still very much a real, traumatic event in their lives. They needed psychological support. Half of them, in fact, needed even more intensive support, since they were still experiencing the disaster as a real event with continuing consequences.

We were able to conclude that our results with the LifeLook program showed that core therapeutic tasks can be achieved by children through interacting with the program – with the assistance of (even briefly) trained mental health professionals. In addition to helping a child progress through the stages of coping, LifeLook helped with five core problems related to distorted feelings about expectations of life arising from a traumatic event. These are: (a) feeling that their lives will be cut short, (b) a tendency to paint a dark, mental picture of the past or future, (c) emptiness about the present, (d) a sense of unrealized possibilities, and (e) a feeling of lack of prospects.

We examined ways of using LifeLook and found that by having trauma victims view their lives from differing perspectives and reassessing these perspectives as they are challenged to do so by the LifeLook program, children can move along from the early stages of coping to near or complete resolution. In doing so, the program helps them reduce the dominance of the traumatic event both in their present lives and in their expectations for the future. Examples of how this has been achieved are presented in the following sections.

Correcting the Life Schedule in Children Feeling Their Lives Will Be Cut Short

In the "expectation of consequences of the disaster" phase, concern about effects of the traumatic event on health and uncertain prospects for the distant future led some children to plan to realize most of the important events in their lives before the age of 25. Table 8 shows a list of meaningful events from 15-year-old Timur which he wrote on November 1, 1991.

Table 8. List of life events from Timur, age 15.

Dates	Events	Age (years)
June 7, 1975	Birth	0
October 11, 1982	Brother's birth	7
April 26, 1986	The disaster	10
September 1, 1990	New school	15
1992	Trip	16
June 1, 1992	Oustanding health	16
July 31, 1992	University	17
June 1993	Trip to the United States	17
June 1, 1995	Wedding	19
1996	Car	20
1997	Interesting job	21
May 1997	House	21
2000	Discoveries	24
2020	Space flight	44
2090	Death	144

Timur hoped to see and do everything a person could normally expect out of a whole lifetime in the former USSR, but in the course of only eight years: a trip to the USA, a house, a car, an interesting job, a discovery, and a peaceful family life. The only thing he did not anticipate was the birth of a child, which may be an indication of his fears of adverse fertility consequences from radiation exposure.

Compare Timur's life schedule with a typical schedule for Kiev high school seniors one year before the disaster, based on data from sociological surveys.[120] Timur planned to marry and find an interesting job 6-8 years earlier than his Kiev peers from 1985; having his own home and a car came 10-12 years earlier; and making a scientific discovery came 11 years earlier. Timur seemed in a hurry to live. In fact, after the age of 25 he had no plans on earth, and all that was left was flying into space. As to his hopes of longevity, this was probably a compensation for the real anxiety he had about his health, brought on by a heightened sense of life's limitations drawn from his experience of the accident.

How can we help in such a situation? First, the acute sense of mortality must be altered. The "life has no limits" technique in the LifeLook program may be used here. After completing independent work with the program, the student was asked to return to the "events" procedure and, in place of the event "birth," to write some event of significance to him that occurred before his birth; and in place of "death," an event that would occur after his death. These two "marker" events could be connected with the lives of his immediate family, distant relatives, or the history of the country as a whole.

After this, it is useful to give a young person in a hurry to live, encouragement to relax and reconsider his crowded plans, to decide which of the planned events he can and perhaps should postpone to a later date, say, ages 30, 35 or 40. This would give him a possibility of an alternative perspective of his life – one that can be lived richly and longer than feared. Perhaps there can be time arranged not only for a marriage, but time also to have a family life, including children. Such therapeutic work is possible because the LifeLook program can be used to return to any of its procedures and make changes as deemed appropriate.

Training to Replace Pessimistic (Dark) Thinking with a Positive View of the Future

Maxim, a ninth grader, had a very pessimistic view of the future. He gave the disaster a great deal of significance, ranking it as the second most important event in his life. Table 9 shows Maxim's list of meaningful events and the colors he associated with them.

Maxim colored most post-explosion events in colors he did not like (blue, black, and gray). Even those events in which he might have taken pride, such as defending a little boy and saving a drowning person, were unpleasant for him. We called such a negative influence of the traumatic event on subsequent life a "darkening" of the future. Psychological help given in such cases must be directed first at encouraging the child to think optimistically. The following techniques were used to accomplish this:

1. Finding positive consequences of the traumatic event as opposed to simply negative consequences. In response to this chal-

Table 9. List of life events from Maxim, age 14.

Dates	Events	Age (years)	Color
September 1, 1982	Entering School	5.5	Red
April 26, 1986	Chernobyl explosion	9	Black
June 1986	Move	9	Brown
June 1991	Defended a little boy	14	Blue
August 11, 1991	Grandmother's death	14	Black
September 1, 1992	Enter technical school	15	Red
June 1995	Change apartments	18	Violet
Fall 1995	Enter the army	18	Gray
September 1997	My job	20	Blue
June 1998	Buy a car	21	Yellow
Winter 1999	Save a drowning person	21	Gray
October 1999	My children	22	Violet
March 2000	Mother dies	22	Black
July 2000	Sister marries	23	Red
August 2000	Father dies	23	Black

Note: Colors in order of preference are green, violet, red, yellow, brown, blue, black, gray.

lenge, Maxim filled his list with such joys of life as a trip to Cuba (one year before), buying a moped (one year after), getting married (at 23) and finally, at 25, moving from a boring job to an interesting and more challenging one.

2. Connecting events related to the loss of loved ones with additional events that, in a sense, serve to continue their lives ("life has no limits"). For instance: encouraging thoughts about the birth and successes of grandchildren who may share characteristics of grandparents who might not have fared well after the trauma.

3. Finding occasions to challenge and praise the child, showing sincere surprise and delight at brave things he has done (defending...) and is ready to do (saving...). After such positive feedback, one can then propose to Maxim that he look again at his coloring of events to see if he sees things any differently.

4. Reinforcing a positive attitude toward the future. The program can automatically propose reconsidering goals and reasons for additional and more pleasant events.

These techniques may help children consider at once two separate realities: the unresolved trauma-organized reality, colored

negatively by an all-dominant trauma, compared to fantasies of a future in which the trauma is less dominant, and there may be bright colors and positive emotions that can coexist alongside serious consequences of the dark trauma. As a result, the children have the option of choosing (at least in play) the second reality of having a brighter perception of the future. In doing so, they begin to pay more attention to what they consider to have been more pleasant times in their respective lives, despite the dark times.

"Meetings with Miracles" in Place of Darkening of the Past

One of the stages in experiencing a traumatic event is the loss of the event's intrusive potential when the consequences are, in the perceiver's opinion, exhausted. The person begins to relate to the event in a calm, moderate manner, but the price for this calm varies by how it has been achieved.

After people were evacuated from the contaminated areas surrounding Chernobyl, they were not infrequently faced with a difficult choice. Is it better 1) to reject the past, together with all the bright memories of life before the disaster, and start a new, hopefully better life from scratch, or instead is it better 2) to keep the memories of golden times and risk the disappointment that the present and, perhaps, even the future may not be as good as the past?

If the present contains hope, rejecting the past is the easier of the two, but before one can reject the past, the past must be painted in appropriately gloomy tones. This is precisely what gave rise to the phenomenon of darkening memories of the past seen in some children.

Vitaly, age 14, who had been in Pripyat at the time of the disaster, moved to Kiev in the fall of 1986. Table 10 presents Vitaly's view of his chief life events five years after disaster.

Vitaly's darkening of the past is shown here by his complete denial of his pre-school childhood. All he called to memory was death and illnesses. He even colored an event before his birth (his father's job) in gray, his least favorite color. Vitaly accepted his life after the disaster almost in its entirety. He related to the near future seriously but optimistically. Most of his plans concerned study, work and family life.

Table 10. List of life events from Vitaly, age 14.

Dates	Events	Age (years)	Color
1965	Fathers's job	11 before birth	Gray
1976	My illness	1	Gray
1978	Grandmother dies	2	Black
1980	Grandfather dies	4	Black
1983	Started school	7	Yellow
April 26, 1986	Explosion	9	Blue
November 1986	Moving to Kiev	10	Violet
July 1988	Sister starts university	12	Green
1989	Friendship with peers	12	Red
1990	School experience	13	Blue
September 28, 1990	Traveled abroad	14	Green
1991	Relations with family	14	Blue
June 1993	Entering technical school	17	Yellow
1999	Starting work	22	Yellow
April 2001	Getting married	24	Violet

Note: Colors in order of preference are violet, green, blue, red, black, yellow, brown, gray.

Vitaly has disconnected the disaster from his future. The disaster does not particularly traumatize him, because in a sense, he has disowned it, but he has also disowned the richness of his past village, family and community life. On the positive side, because of the disaster, he moved to the big city, took a trip abroad, and his sister went to the university. On the other hand, he has lost all the wonder and joy of his childhood, particularly one that was closely connected to the land and nature. One might say that Vitaly has sacrificed his childhood self along with his spontaneous and free creativity from earlier life, in exchange for the present sobriety with which he now views life.

To help Vitaly recapture some of the wonder that he relinquished with disowning his childhood wonder, which he may need if he is to experience life to the fullest, the psychotherapist may use the "meeting a miracle" technique. In the opinion of G. S. Altshuller, author of an original theory on resolving problems with inventive solutions, "meeting a miracle" is an obligatory event in the childhood of all accomplished inventors.[121]

The child is asked to remember some unusual event that struck his imagination, astonishing him with its beauty and uniqueness; something that could be termed a minor "miracle." For one child, this miracle may have been the splendor of a holiday celebration; while for another, the miracle may have been a first encounter with the sea. For yet another, it could be the discovery of how to repair a broken alarm clock or a computer. It is good when the child remembers several such encounters. The earlier in the healing process that they are evoked, the more productive they may become in the child's rehabilitation process.

The "miracles" are added to the list of life events and may be used to replace unpleasant memories from childhood already entered into the LifeLook program. After asking a child to construct a list of miracles, one must explain the connection between "meeting with a miracle" and other life events, by once more going through the "goals," "causes," and "significances" procedures. For example, despite Chernobyl, daffodils continue to bloom each spring. This gives the child the opportunity to again view two realities: the harsh coldness that may defend him from being hurt by the trauma, as well as seeing the trauma in the context of other small miracles that are neither diminished nor erased by the darkness of the trauma. While struggling with the destructive influence of a dark trauma, the child is reintroduced to his own awe, in a creative process which he may accept as coexisting with the equally-powerful forces of destruction. The restorative power of focusing on small wonders encountered in life is a powerful counterbalance to the weighty, darkening power of the traumatic event.

Awareness of "Super" Significant Events in Individuals Feeling Emptiness About the Present

Experiences connected with a disaster have varying influences on children's life expectations. Some experiences caused them to focus less on lofty success and more on making their key goals: normal health, good living conditions, and recognition from friends and loved ones. Other children, who were more determined to avoid future suffering, found traumatic events to be stimulants, propelling them toward goals that bring acclaim, glory, respect and the acknowledgment of posterity. For those trying to push past limits imposed by the trauma, the sharp contrast between high expectations and the real conditions of the day can make the current period of life lose its value, leading to a sense of emptiness about the present.

Emptiness in the present is most easily detected using LifeLook when looking at the results of the "five-year period" procedure. A feeling of emptiness in the present was revealed by a kind of "hole" in the life graph,[122] such as when 15-year-old Svetlana viewed the eventfulness of five-year periods of her life (see Figure 8).

Svetlana who was 10 years old at the time of the Chernobyl accident, saw her first two five-year periods as being rather eventful. Then came the emptiness of the current five-years, and the minimal richness of the next few (see Figure 8A). After running the five-year period procedure, LifeLook recommended that Svetlana seek psychological counseling. Psychological help for those children suffering from feelings of emptiness in the present may be based on techniques that search out highly significant life meanings or events as follows:

1. Some memories and expectations are so central and important to a person, so close to him/her, that they are not at first identified.

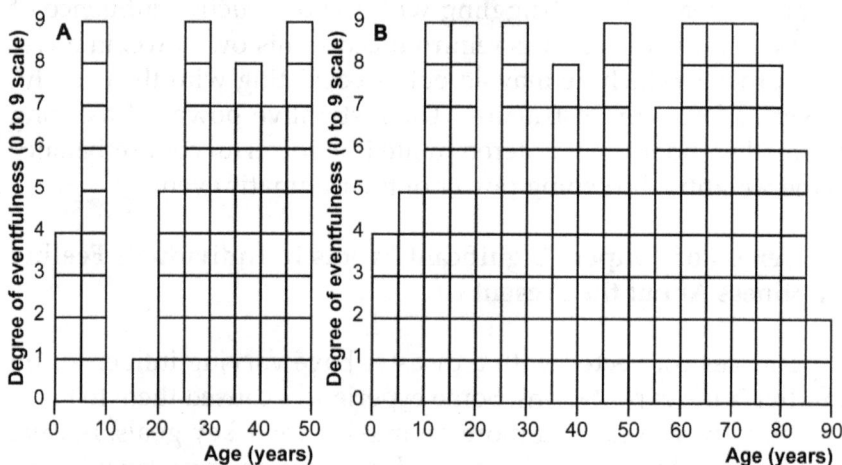

Figure 8. Estimates of eventfulness of five-year periods, when suffering from feelings of emptiness in the present (Svetlana, age 15). A = before psychotherapy; B = after psychotherapy.

When Svetlana was asked to find the "super" significant events and to record them on the screen, she replied, "It was a family secret." It turned out that her family had found it necessary to hide the nobility of her mother's side of the family during Communist times. When this was discovered recently, Svetlana felt her social value enhanced. She included this discovery in her list, and after analyzing the connections between her list of events, it carried the highest motivational status.

2. The technique of seeking personally-meaningful events dating from before one's birth and after one's anticipated death based on the "life has no limits" principle also gives an opportunity to redefine the significance of all life experience, and potentially remediate places where life is seen as empty. Svetlana found two such events, i.e. "grandmother's honor" (an honor present 70 years before Svetlana's birth) and "remembrances." Namely, she fantasized about a film in which she would participate, be known for and seen even 10-20 years after her death.

3. Erasing those aspects of life that are chance elements, which are more revealing of life's hustle and bustle than of anything truly worth considering is also a way to overcome one's feeling of emptiness. "Erase the accidental traits – And you will see: the world is beautiful", as poet Alexander Blok wrote[123]. Svetlana found several such things that could be eliminated from her list of events: "kung fu lessons," "first kiss," "fight," and "being pretty" (she is already pretty). This made room on the list for more meaningful events.

4. Acknowledging the great role to be played by new, additional events in the course of analyzing their goals, reasons, and place in the hierarchy of values and on the map of life helps relieve a person's feelings of emptiness. To enable him or her instead to find meaning in the present requires a great deal of tact, patience, and confidence that such meaning can, and will be found. With challenges provided in the program, enduring changes in perspective often do occur, even in a short space of time.

The effectiveness of the help may be evaluated by a second administration of the "five-year period" procedure after therapeutic work. Svetlana's repeat life graph, created approximately two hours after the first graph, is also shown in Figure 8B.

As may be seen here, Svetlana's relations with life changed considerably, and the present is full of significant experiences. This change occurred in a relatively short span of time, as she was challenged to reevaluate and potentially make richer choices as to how she anticipated her life unfolding.

Acknowledging Good Experiences in the Past as a Means Toward Claiming a Fuller Future

The realization of a person's life intentions may be measured through the relative weight given to the past, in one's overall view of life. The more realization there is, the more psychologically mature the person is, and vice-versa. The optimal value for realization is when the psychological age[124] corresponds most closely to chronological age. When the psychological age is seven or more years below the chronological age, the program generates a recommendation for counseling.

Devaluation of past attainments and life experiences can, and often does, lead to a severe lack of fulfillment. An example may be found in the life graph of Larisa, age 14 (see Figure 9A).

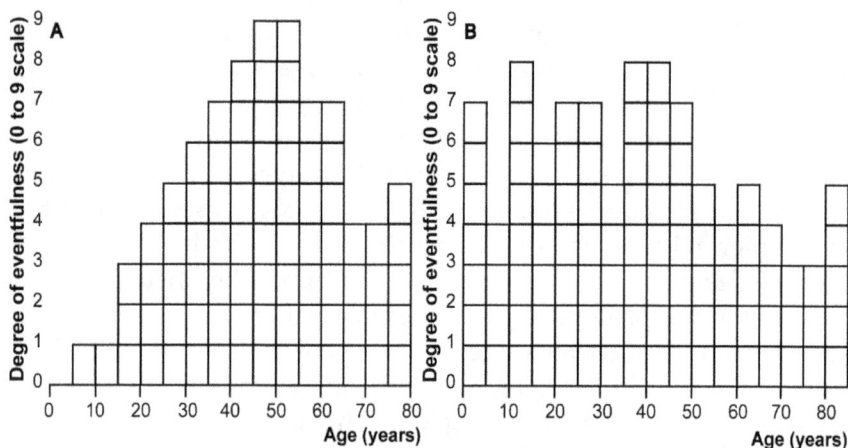

Figure 9. Estimates of eventfulness of five-year periods, when suffering from feelings of lack of fulfillment (Larisa, age 14). A = before psychotherapy; B = after psychotherapy.

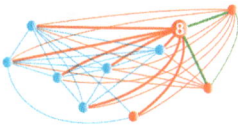

Larisa viewed nothing in her past as valuable. She placed only two unconnected events: "grandmother" in her first year of life and "Pripyat" on April 26, 1986, in her past. In Larisa's opinion, "Pripyat" had many consequences for her future and, therefore, was experienced by her as a very unfinished event, an event in the psychological present – important for her today. Since the experience had not been psychologically resolved, it interfered with her ability to enjoy the present and to evaluate the past, thereby retarding psychological growth. The following techniques may be used as therapeutic measures:

1. Searching for positive, significant events that occurred before the accident, as well as afterward, can change how the entire trauma is viewed in dictating the course of one's life. Some of these positive events may be unexpected consequences of the accident, thereby lowering its negative impact and dominance in dictating a negative life outcome. Finding positive outcomes as well as negative ones may lead to a total reconsideration of life expectations.

2. Include these autobiographical "finds" in the overall list of events at the same time that the child is encouraged to consider fantasizing about erasing some expectations of illness, loss, and their associated anxieties.

3. After an analysis of reasons and goals, discuss with the child the changed life map, emphasizing achievements.

This alone can create a changed life map that begins to emphasize at least some degree of control and achievements that had previously gone unrecognized.

In psychotherapeutic work with Larisa, she revived pleasant memories of how she had gone to school before the accident and traveled to Kiev where she saw her younger sister for the first time. She also remembered how she had vacationed on the Crimean seacoast after the accident. Subsequent to the psychotherapy, Larisa looked to the future with greater optimism, imagining the birth of nephews (instead of the death of her parents) and of grandchildren (instead of her own death). Larisa's post-therapy life graph (right side of Figure 9) differed significantly from the original. The second one revealed far less lack of fulfillment. The past was now represented as having been richer than simply being dominated by the experience of the disaster.

What to Do about Feeling There Is a Lack of Prospects?

Finding one's calling is always difficult, especially when a past trauma continues to cast a shadow on the future. Some of the boys and girls who experienced the Chernobyl disaster preferred not to look into the immediate future. Instead, they acquired a tendency to "go with the flow" in their school years. More often than not, that "flow" led from one stress to another: from the disaster itself to difficulties such as adapting to a new place and from separation to disenchantment. Such on-going stress and trauma may result in a general mistrust of life, uncertainty in oneself and one's future.

It has been observed that when these children work with the LifeLook program, they do not look far into the future and, typically, only produce one or two events they imagine will occur relatively soon. Even when these children do imagine future events, they seldom (and only tentatively) connect them to events from their past life. During therapeutic work, these children have trouble naming events further into the future, usually limiting themselves to the traditional events of family life. When these cognitive constructs are cast against a background of feeling a lack of prospects, the future seems very tenuously connected to the child's past life. This is true even with things the child loves. Galina's lifemap at age 15, (Figure 6, page 66), is an illustration of this condition. She named only one future event, "brother" at number 14. All of the other events were placed in the future only after the psychologist asked her to thoughtfully reconsider the future. As we observed, the prospects were not very meaningful, and more importantly, not at all connected with the past.

Children who feel they are without prospects are more in need of intensive, long-term psychotherapy, the goal of which is to help them develop the ability to think creatively about their own future. This form of psychological help may be termed "lessons in lifecraft," and may require more extensive interaction and challenges with the program than these limited interventions provide.

The lessons in lifecraft have been designed for 10 weekly sessions of 60-90 minutes each, and they may be organized as extra-curricular activities for high school students.[125] The general goal of these activities is acquainting adolescents with the basic ideas of

life-span psychology in order to develop self-analysis skills and, ultimately, the ability to shape one's own life. They learn how to use LifeLook so they can return to it on their own, as a self-help psychological tool.

Not a Panacea but Worth a Try

Are the psychological distortions in the LifeLook profiles reported unique to the children exposed to the Chernobyl disaster? Are they typical only for these children, or do they also apply to many people who have experienced trauma? Clearly, current theories of psychological trauma reflected in the diagnostic criteria for PTSD[126] include as symptoms feelings of a foreshortened future, distortions in experience of time associated with intrusive memories, and re-experiencing of traumatic memories as key features of the post-traumatic state.[127] Researchers McCann & Pearlman[128], among others, have likewise documented the trauma-induced shattering of the assumptive world, including expectations for the future.

In assessing other groups, we found similar distortions in distressed populations (79% of handicapped adults, 56% of mental health clinic clients, and 13% of a control group)[129] tested using LifeLook procedures. Adolescents living without parents in an orphanage also reported feelings of unrealized possibilities, emptiness, and/or lack of prospects 67% of the time.[130]

So what are the possible consequences of uncorrected distortions in individuals exposed to the Chernobyl disaster? These can include negative influences on their health, leading to socially maladaptive behavior, and impairment of the sociopsychological climate in society as whole, especially as more individuals become affected.[131] Even before the Chernobyl accident, Russian adolescents displayed a close connection between distortion of their view of life and pessimistic expectations of longevity, on the one hand, and between positive attitudes toward alcoholic beverages and deviant behavior on the other.[132]

New evidence for this premise has appeared since Chernobyl. Recall that, in 1986, Pripyat-evacuated teenagers expected to live 8.3 fewer years than their peers from Kiev[133], and rescue teams who worked within a 30-km (18.6 mi) radius of the nuclear plant estimated their lifetime as 5 to 9 years shorter than other, same-aged men in the former USSR.[134] From 1985-94, the number of suicides in Kiev doubled from the previous nine years. (Kiev is only 101 km (63 miles) from Chernobyl, and in the weeks following the explosion, all the children of Kiev were also advised to temporarily evacuate.)

A study of 4,742 Estonian "liquidators", one group out of more than 600,000 men who heroically shut down and cleaned the nuclear reactor and surrounding areas to reduce further contamination, revealed that the leading cause of death was not cancer, but rather suicide.[135] Similarly, the number of suicides within a 60-km (37.4 mi) radius of the Semipalatinsk nuclear test site in Kazakhstan was four times higher than in the nearby region.[136]

It is unrealistic to expect that millions of people living in the contaminated areas will totally escape negative physical effects. Illnesses from radiation are tragic, but even more so is the despair and stress-induced illnesses and suicides that a trauma-organized view of the future may breed. Even many years after the disaster, the affected children will require continuing psychological support to cope with permanent stress and help to create a positive view of their lives.

Even with the large numbers of individuals involved and the economic hardships of the region, it is nevertheless possible for interventions of the type LifeLook provided, to be implemented with little additional staffing or cost to the already crumbling social systems.

Is the LifeLook technique effective over a long period of time, or can it eliminate psychological distortions in the short run only? The answer can come only after a second set of longitudinal studies. However, some evidence for the effectiveness of this approach already exists. Working with mental health clinic adult clients in Siberia, Akhmerov demonstrated the long-term effectiveness of some coping techniques related to the feeling of lack of prospects. Assessments one month after group training and, again, six months later showed that clients indicated that their future time perspectives were more productive, and their lifetime expectations were more optimistic.[137]

Thus, despite the absence of direct longitudinal data, other studies suggest that the LifeLook approach for psychological sup-

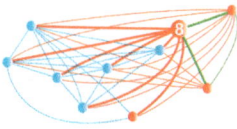

port of the adolescent victims of the Chernobyl disaster will have long-term effectiveness. These children will have been able to, at least, develop a creative attitude toward their own lives, as well as a caring attitude about other people's lives.

It is difficult for children to preserve such a socially constructive attitude toward life against the background of significant, traumatic events and ecological disasters. This makes it all the more important that special psychological programs be placed in schools to help children cope with life's crises, adapt their views of the future when such traumas do occur, and develop an approach to life that is both productive and successful, a joy for the individuals as well as for their loved ones.

Other Uses of LifeLook

What other populations might benefit from such an approach? The potential applications of this program for other adolescent populations are many. Children who have faced exposure to toxic materials or evacuated from their homes due to either natural and manmade disasters—from a hurricane to the outbreak of war—are likely to benefit from working through their trauma-organized orientations to the future.

Perhaps the most powerful application of this technique could be for inner city youth, especially those exposed to widespread physical violence, AIDs, STDs, verbal and mental abuse, and the fear they will not survive, or will be imprisoned. They have a high risk of believing in a foreshortened lifespan. Although far removed from their Pripyat counterparts, many poor, urban youths struggle with the uncertainty of violence releasing its own kind of poison into their futures.

We believe that a tool such as LifeLook could be implemented in schools with tangible results, at relatively little cost. The LifeLook intervention strategy cannot altogether replace classical approaches to understanding and treating post-traumatic stress disorder.[138] But when resources are limited and entire populations are in need of effective and efficient intervention, this tool may be implemented with the likelihood of improving the quality of people's lives.

Biographical Computer Games

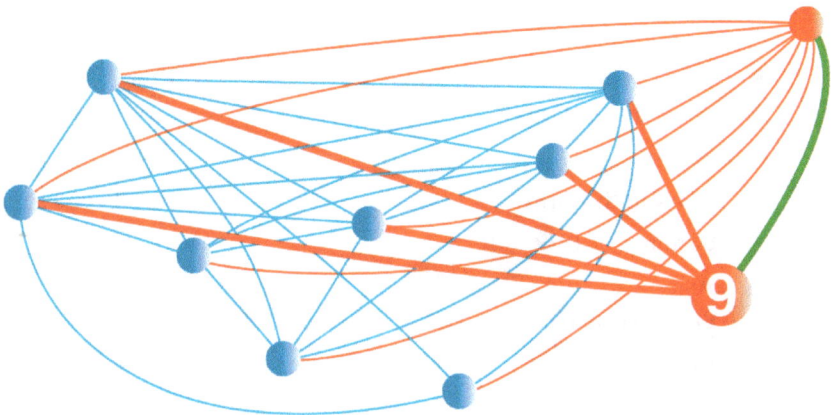

Even more circumspect people realize that it is not possible to live without play. Pianist Sviatoslav Richter devised the game *A Musician's Journey* to have participants experience the practice, mistakes, memories, vows, betrayals, and prizes in the life of a musician.[139] This type of biographical game has become increasingly popular.

Just as theater imitates life, life games like fortune-telling or sorcery help people live their lives. Traditional game pieces, such as cards, help fortune-tellers analyze the patterns of a person's life. Additional technology allows us all to design our own destiny.

In 1986, a computer program entitled *Biographer* was developed for psychobiographical research (a later version called LifeLook is described in Chapters 7, 8 and 10). Users can analyze main events from their past, present, and future, as well as causes and goals of their actions to discover the significance of each event and to create a map of their life course. This program can be used as a basis for the developing of various computer games. Here are a few scripts.

Sage

Within *Biographer*, the game of *Sage* lets a person view life events on the screen in chronological order using the player's own words, such as in Figure 10.

- First impression
- Arrival in the capital
- School
- Work in the farm
- Summer of 1939
- Asia
- Start of WWII
- Missile
- Department chairperson
- Marriage
- Birth of daughters
- Success
- Peace

Figure 10. List of life events in the game of *Sage*.

Sage then instructs the player to choose "significant events, which have most changed your life, or will in the future." Suppose that "First impression" is chosen. *Sage* will then inform the player, "You are somewhat mistaken. This event should be placed third in importance. Which event should be first?"

The program has counted the number of connections the user previously attributed to each event. A person can sometimes fail to attribute importance to critical events, but *Sage* is objective. So, which event should be placed first? You try again. "Start of the war." *Sage* responds, "You are close to the truth, but this event is of secondary importance to you. Which should be placed in the foremost position?"

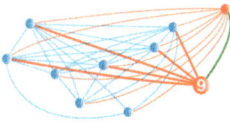

Finally, when you answer "Peace," you receive the awaited verdict: "You are absolutely correct. This event is first in significance. Now think a bit – which event should be fourth?" The game continues until the ranking is complete. The screen then shows the results, as seen in Figure 11.

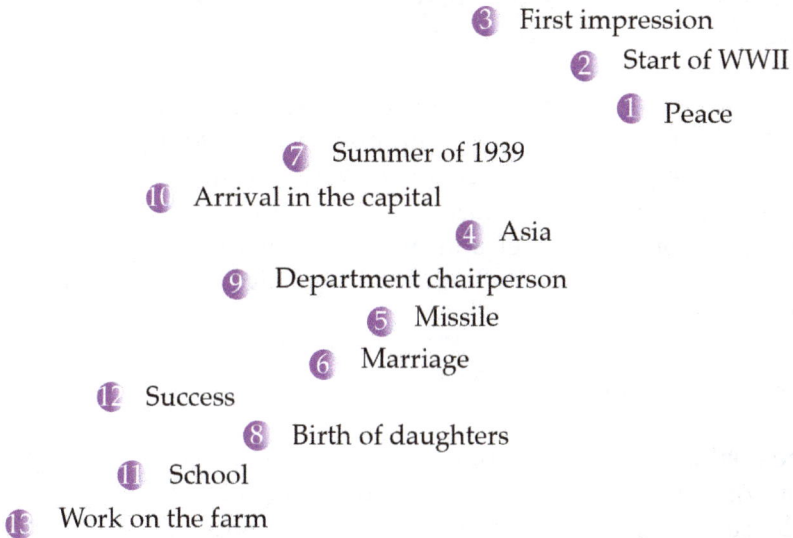

3 First impression

2 Start of WWII

1 Peace

7 Summer of 1939

10 Arrival in the capital

4 Asia

9 Department chairperson

5 Missile

6 Marriage

12 Success

8 Birth of daughters

11 School

13 Work on the farm

Figure 11. High level of realism in the game of *Sage*.

While you have arranged the events from top to bottom according to their importance, *Sage* has positioned them from right to left, assigning the number 1 to the most significant event it chose. If your evaluation is identical to *Sage*'s, the events will appear in a perfectly diagonal order from the upper right corner to the bottom left corner.

The degree of proximity of your arrangement to a perfect diagonal is an index of the degree of realism for your view of life. It is measured in points, from -100 to +100. A negative number is given to those with difficulty deciding the most significant events in life. A positive number characterizes those who think relatively clearly and evaluate events realistically. On average, only a third of the players scored more than sixty points.

Incognito

Another biographical game, *Incognito,* can be seen as a sort of "human destiny bank." An actual (anonymous) person's most important life events, dates, gender, and date of birth appear on a screen. Also displayed are experienced and expected events. You must guess which date or age coincides with the most important event. If you are mistaken, the event will remain a mystery. The process is then repeated. As a result, a list of ages and events is displayed on the screen in order of their importance, from your point of view.

Still, the game is not complete. Your insight is measured using points: for the first phase, 20 for each correct response, then fewer, as you guess over and over. The idea was for *Incognito* to train your imagination and intuition to relate to the perceptions of other people.

The Game of Destiny

The goal is to construct your life course using only your imagination. At the bottom of the screen, your imaginary life is displayed – like a long ribbon, divided into five-year segments, from the first to the last impression. At first, the segments are empty. You are instructed to fill these vacant segments with events. The events appear in different positions along the upper border of the screen, falling toward the bottom of the screen at various speeds ("raining down on your life"). You move the ribbon to the left and to the right, finding places for the events as they fall. The events can be pleasant, unpleasant, or vague. Their significance is determined by their neighboring events, in the midst of which they fall. Whether the event is first love, insight, a new career, or the death of a friend, your assignment is to create an interesting, rich, and harmonious biography.

Your biography is then evaluated against a standard. The first criterion is based first on the distribution of pleasant and unpleasant events. An extended "dark period" can undermine a person's ability to live and may lead to additional unhappiness. On the other hand, a lengthy "cheerful period" can weaken a person, and may contribute to defenselessness in the face of adversity.

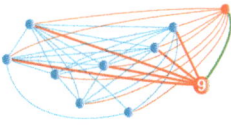

The second criterion is the harmonious mixture of business, family, and spiritual life. If, during a period of life, you are dedicated to attaining just one goal, for example, the program suggests that your life will be impoverished and your personality deformed.

The third criterion is the timely occurrence of common events (e.g. marriage and a promotion at work). Sociologists claim that a considerable divergence from the desired date of such events could lead to unwanted stress.[140]

Each "imbalance" in the game of *Destiny* has an impact on a person's strength, health, experiences, and length of life. A series of difficult periods could tragically interrupt a person's young life, but finding an optimal strategy will enable a player to reach biblical age.

Your Own Face

The widespread development of biographical games involving computer characters to play along with us is an interesting trend. In the game called *Your Own Face*, you and four characters travel along parallel, horizontal lines as your life progresses. A face capable of changing expression – sad or happy, naïve or cunning, energetic or passive – is assigned to each player (see Figure 12 on page 96).

With your computer characters as companions, you advance along the path of life, each character's facial expression influencing neighboring faces (including yours). The goal is to attain a particular facial expression at the end of the path.

How can this goal be attained? Only one solution is permitted – proceed through life by changing paths via vertical lines that serve as bridges. When this occurs, you have different neighboring faces that can also change paths and expressions but cannot coerce you to change your place.

The first phase of the game concludes when the end of the screen is reached. The feedback is a purposeful facial expression.

In the second phase (childhood), the computer characters are divided into friends and enemies. Friendly characters are similar to each other, while enemies are dissimilar. The goal remains the same – to attain the desired expression.

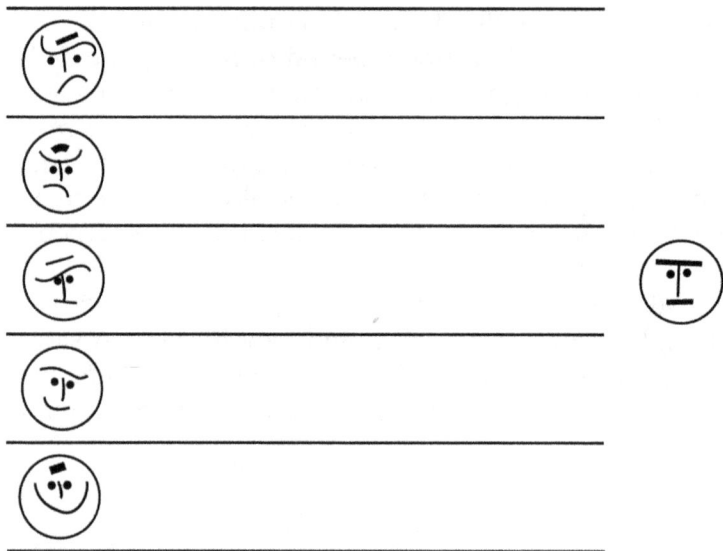

Figure 12. Find your expression along the path of your life.

During the third stage, male and female characters appear but the rules of mutual influence are more complex. For example, a male face is identical in appearance to a friendly female face and a male enemy, but dissimilar to a friendly male face and a female enemy, so it is more complicated to attain the desired facial expression.

In the adult life phase, the desired expression of "your face" is, at first, unknown, but is revealed at the end.

Traveler

The games described above are all parts of the larger game called *Traveler*, where players find themselves at crossroads in their lives, and must choose which direction to go. They may encounter friends or enemies, even accidental events. However, behavior and events are also partly determined by their decisions. The goal of the game is to live a harmonious and full life. Each phase of the game is evaluated by the criteria of personal happiness, business productivity, and public goodwill.

Causometry, Lech Lecha Challenge and Cognitive Modifiability: How to Build a Bridge from the Psychological Past to the Future

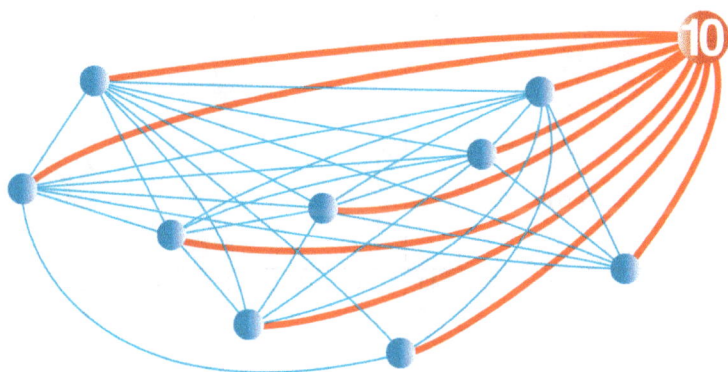

My first co-authored article in 1973 was about Lev Vygotsky, his ideas of psychological tools and the mediated nature of the higher mental processes.[141] Since that time, in tandem with many brilliant colleagues, I have developed several such tools, and we have introduced a constructivist definition of the human mind/ psyche.[142] Now, it refers to a mode of a person's orientation in the world and relations with the world, which is being constantly created and updated, owing to the high plasticity of the human nervous system.

One of the psychological tools developed by our group was the causometry software program LifeLook.[143] Causometry is the method for analyzing the personal image of time as an amalgamation of one's significant life events and various causal and goal relationships between events, i.e., a multi-layer time composition of the memories of one's past, experiences of one's present, and expectations of one's future.[144] The idea is that the human experience of time depends on the way significant life events are perceived to be connected with one another.[145] A causogram is a graphic representation of the events and their interconnections in the form of a "digraph" (directional graph), as seen in Figure 13.

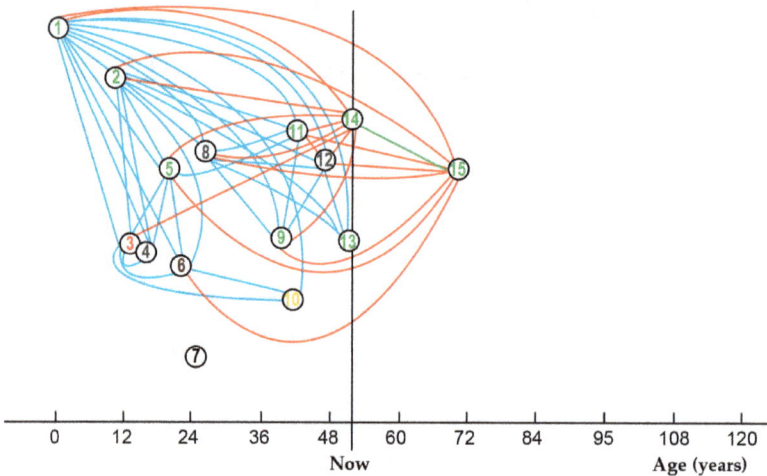

Figure 13. The first version of Natan's causogram.

Fifteen small rectangles indicate different events in the life of 49-year-old Natan, a devoted educator. Blue lines indicate Natan's thoughts about motivational connections between his past events (realized connections); green lines indicate connections between his possible future events (potential connections); and red lines connect past events with future events (actual or topical connections). This 2011 graph was only the first version of his causogram.

Natan likened the causogram to a GPS in one's life journey. The 11th version of his causogram more than two years later, after several sessions using LifeLook is seen in Figure 14. He nicknamed the program, "the causometry machine."

Different cognitive-motivational structural characteristics of one's life vision are illustrated in Table 11 with their interpretations in the Appendix. The first four indexes are the Motivational Intensity of the psychological past, present, future, and life as a whole.

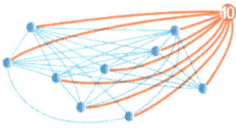

Another index is the Sense of Reality. The more connections an event has, the higher its location on the causogram. The weighted sum of connections indicates the Motivational Status of the event,

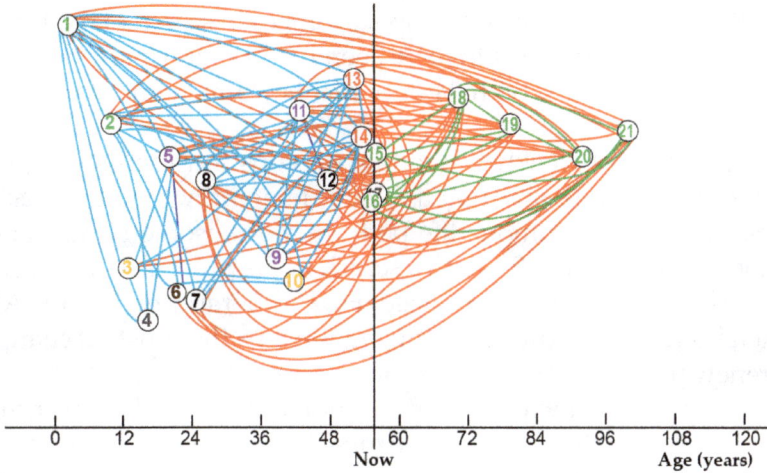

Figure 14. The eleventh version of Natan's causogram.

i.e., the real significance of this event in one's life. The hierarchy of all events by their motivational status may be closer to or farther from their hierarchy by subjective, direct, verbal, conscious ranking of importance of these events in one's life. The correlation of these

Table 11. Causometric indexes related to the causogram on Figure 14.

Characteristics	Past	Present	Future	Total
Motivational Intensity	37.9%	49.4%	12.7%	47.5%
Goal-Directedness	46.3%	35.1%	43.3%	40.4%
Difficulty	1.3%	0.0%	0.0%	0.5%
Rationality	82.9%	88.1%	92.4%	86.4%
Strategy-Oriented	13.5L	34.7L	4.7L	52.8L
Confidence	73.6%	70.9%	57.1%	70.7%
Life Satisfaction	47.5%	66.4%	88.7%	62.0%
Emotionality	63.6%	79.9%	91.0%	75.1%
Sense of Reality				79

two hierarchies (multiplied by 100) is the index of Total Sense of Reality in Table 11 (see more in Appendix).

"Lech Lecha"[146], a classic call in the *Torah*, could be translated into modern English as "Go to your true self." Most of today's clients, I think, come to psychotherapists' offices in search of their true selves. At least, so it seems to have been in my first American experience from 2001-2008, with 34 outpatients: 25 men and 9 women, ages 13-83.

On average, 34 weekly individual sessions were conducted, including the LifeLook program as a supplementary tool. *Lech Lecha* means a search for a unique life path, so the causometry machine, LifeLook, is a good tool for such a search in the process of Metabolic Time-Oriented Computer-Assisted Psychotherapy or M-TOCAP. By metabolic, I mean the psychic metabolism – the constant change and renewal of our mind, psyche or neshama.[147]

This approach includes many therapeutic techniques (introduced in Chapter 8) for a cognitive modification of one's life vision: correcting the life schedule in those who feel that their lives will be cut short, training to replace pessimistic (darkening) thinking with a positive view of the future, awareness of "super" significant events in individuals with feelings of emptiness about the present, acknowledging good experiences in the past as a means of claiming a fuller future, life-craft lessons, etc.[148] From small revisions, new versions of causograms evolve with new, updated psycho-biographical causometric indexes on different stages of psychotherapy (see Table 12).

Stage A could be named "Insight & Strengthening Sense of Reality." The Sense of Reality (correlation of motivational status with subjective importance of the events) is much higher in the second version of the causogram. In a few sessions, a person becomes wiser and more accurate in his or her assessment of life priorities and in distinguishing between more significant and less significant events.

Stage B is about the change of temporal mode from past-focused to present-focused. Motivational Intensity of the present rises significantly; the previously, mostly bluish causogram becomes more reddish (with more actual connections), and the bridge between the past and future is much wider now.

In stage C, this bridge becomes longer. New long-term perspectives evolve with new expectations from one's future and new re-

Table 12. Changes of causometric indexes on different stages of meta-bolic time-oriented computer-assisted psychotherapy.

Stages	Modifications *Indexes*	Number of revisions of one's causogram
A	Strengthen sense of reality: from smart to wise *Sense of reality, 42 → 58***	1
B	Change temporal mode: from past-focused to present-focused *Motivational intensity of present, 32 → 42**	3
C	Shift strategic thinking: from short-term to long-term *Strategic thinking in present, 3 → 8***	4
D	Renew desire to plan: from retire to restart *Goal-directedness in present, 20 → 36***	5
E	Grow rationally: from Homo sapiens to Homo sapiens sapiens *Rationality in present, 68 → 78**	7
F	Soften view on past: from rigid to flexible *Rigidity in view of past, 89 → 80**	9
G	Appreciate the past: from distresses to lessons *Appreciation of past, 67 → 79**	11

Note: Level of significance by Student's *t*-test.
*p < .05
**p < .01

sources from one's past. As a result, the index of Strategic Thinking in the present is almost three times higher now.

Stage D is marked by a rise of the index of Goal-Directedness in the present. So life on the bridge between the past and future becomes more goal-oriented, less spontaneous.

Stage E is noticeable by the increase of the index of Rationality in the present. Personal life plans are more grounded, and the bridge of the present is more reliable. Now, the much wiser, more present-focused, and more goal-oriented person is ready for a new look into the past.

Stage F is marked by the decrease of Rigidity in views of the past, and stage G, the last one, shows an increase in the index of Appreciation of the past. As a result, the psychological past is transformed from perceived or real distress into a valuable lesson.

Based on my clinical experience and research, steps to build a bridge from the psychological past to the future require cognitive-motivational modifications for the move from being smart to wise, from past-focused to present-focused, from short-term to long-term thinking, from Homo sapiens to Homo sapiens sapiens, from rigid to flexible, and from distresses to lessons.

Psychological time seems to have connections with left/right brain hemispheres, each responsible for processing information mostly about the known past or the unknown future (although data is not the same for right-handed and left-handed people).[149] I believe the corpus callosum is responsible for bridging the psychological past to the future (the red connections). Figure 15 illustrates this hypothesis based on the causogram from Figure 14.

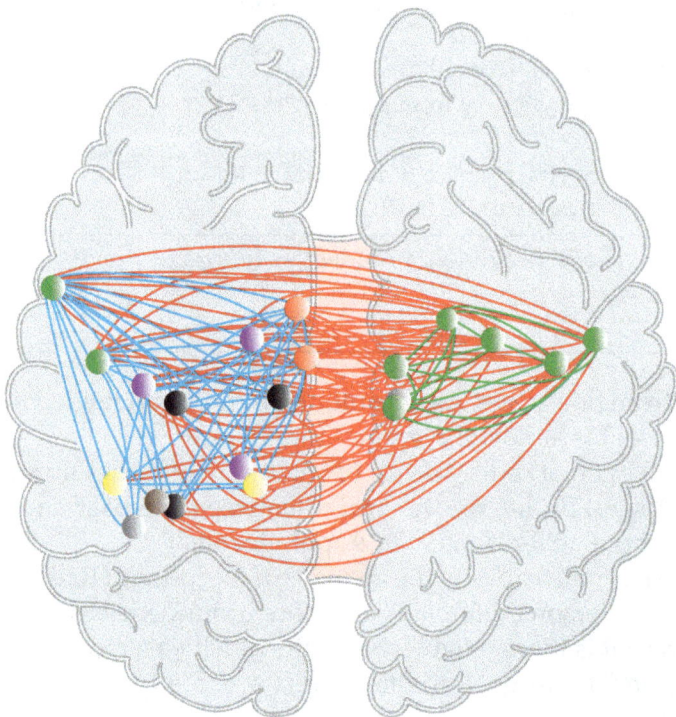

Figure 15. A hypothetical causometric brain.

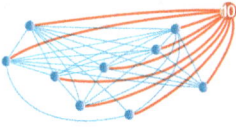

In 1990, I began EEG research for a study of psychological time[150] in Moscow, at the Institute of Psychology of the Russian Academy of Sciences, but was interrupted. Only a few years ago, I learned that also in 1990, Milan Kundera, a well-known Czech writer, wrote in his novel, *Immortality*: "I long for an experiment that would examine, by means of electrodes attached to the human head, exactly how much of one's life a person devotes to the present, how much to the memories, and how much to the future. This would let us know who a man really is in relation to his time. What human time really is."[151]

My hope is that this research will rebuild many bridges from the past to the future.

Epilogue

As I see it now, this book has evolved also from my dad's "puzzle of age." He had changed his formal birth date at the age of fifteen. He was a fifty-plus year-old and already retired army general when I was born. To his last day, no one knew how old he really was. Dad's age was a mystery for me for a long time, yet I never felt I could question him about it. As a result, my own chronological awareness is very flexible and similar to a famous statement of the baseball legend Satchel Paige, "How old would you be if you didn't know how old you are?"[152]

A sense of age is, however, the most important dimension of our human experience of time. It serves as a marker to our personal psychological clock and helps us to navigate successfully through our lifetime journey. It is why everyone needs to solve his or her age puzzle and find a healthy balance between personal past, present and future. In my many years of studying such a puzzle and searching for such balance, I created with my good friends and colleagues a theory of psychological time, a self-help program LifeLook, and a time-oriented computer-assisted psychotherapy. This book is an introduction to these concepts and tools, which can help any open-minded person to navigate his/her psychological time and change his/her unique life story for the better.

"Cherchez la Femme," as the French say. In the home of the amazing Helen Yakobson[153], professor at the George Washington University and, at one time, first anchor at the Voice of America, my family and I spent our first summer in the United States. I left behind, as a gift, an early version of this book in Russian. After six months, Helen suggested having the book translated into English and sponsored the first translation. She was, at that time, nearly 80, and in her words, "Now is the best age of all." Thank you, Helen.

Epilogue

Appendix
Definitions and Interpretations of LifeLook® Indexes

The following psychobiographical indexes of personality can be measured using the professional edition of the computer program, LifeLook,[154] developed in the framework of the goal-and-causal theory of psychological time.[155] Here are brief operational definitions of these indexes, and their possible interpretation in the framework of Dr. Frederick T. Melges' temporal approach to psychiatric disorders.[156] These independently developed approaches have much in common.

1. Motivational intensity MI (min=0, max=100) refers to the fact that a person is asked to indicate (analyze) various motivational – instrumental and causal – connections between each pair of selected events. MI equals the ratio of the sum of all connections indicated by the patient to the maximum possible number of connections.

This index is similar to the concept of "connectivity" used by Melges.[157] Based on Melges' clinical research and my clinical experience, it is reasonable to hypothesize that a very high degree of MI (motivational excessiveness) can be found in paranoid connectivity and a very low degree of MI (motivational insufficiency) in depersonalization.

2. Goal-directedness GD (min=0, max=100) equals the ratio of the sum of instrumental connections to the total sum of instrumental and causal connections. This index is basically the same as "goal-directedness," used by Melges.[158] It is reasonable to assume that a low degree of GD can be found in schizophrenic disorders and a high degree of GD in obsessive-compulsive disorders.

3. Difficulty D (min=0, max=100) equals the ratio of the sum of negative connections (in spite of, to avoid) to the total sum of negative and positive connections. The meaning of this index is close to Melges' concept of "block," "obstacle," and "dread,"[159] though more general. One can assume that a high degree of D can be found in anxiety and depressive disorders and a low degree of D in manic disorders.

4. Rationality Rt (min=0, max=100) equals the ratio of the sum of balanced instrumental connections to the total sum of instrumental connections. This index is similar to the concept of "temporal co-ordination" implied in Melges' approach.[160] It seems reasonable to expect a very low degree of Rt in schizophrenic disorder and a very high degree of Rt in obsessive-compulsive disorders.

5. Strategy St (min=0, max = ∞, but practically limited by 100) equals the sum of instrumental and causal connections considering the duration of temporal intervals between connected events. The meaning of this index is very close to the concept of "continuity" and "identity" in Melges' approach.[161] Based on his observation, one can expect a very high degree of St in paranoid disorders and a very low degree of St in cases of depersonalization.

6. Confidence C (min=0, max=100) equals the sum of confident patient personal answers about how events connect (definitely or independently) to the total sum of connections. The concept of "un-certainty" used by Melges[162] refers to the low level of C common in anxiety disorders. One can expect to find a very high degree of C in paranoid disorders.

7. Life Satisfaction LS (min=0, max=100) is high when a person sees his/her life events in subjectively pleasant colors and low when life events seem to be unpleasant. The concepts of "optimism," "pessimism," used by Melges[163] indicate the same feelings with a focus on personal future. It is reasonable to expect a low degree of LS in depression disorders with suicidal ideation and a high degree of LS in manic episodes.

8. Emotionality E (min=0, max=100) refers to the individual tendency to perceive live events in polar (very pleasant or very unpleasant) colors. Melges used the concept of "intensity of an emotion".[164] Based on his observation, very high intensity of an emotion is non-adaptive while "lesser degrees of emotion appear to facilitate adaptation." From this point of view, it is reasonable to hypothesize a negative correlation between the Global Assessment of Functioning (GAF) scale[165] and the index of emotionality.

9. Sense of Reality SR (min = -100, max = +100) equals the Spearman's quotient (r_s) of correlation (multiplied by 100) between the range of significance assigned to events by a subject and their motivational status. Motivational status equals the number and strength of connections any individual event has with other events. SR can be interpreted as one of the indicators of "reality testing," which is impaired in psychotic disorders (from Melges' point of view) because of significant "temporal disintegration."[166]

10. Psychological Age PA (min=0, max = subjectively expected longevity) is operationally defined as equal to the product of Realization x Years That One Expects to Live. Realization equals the ratio of the psychological past – one's memories – to the sum of the whole. The formula is PA = R x L, where R is realization, and L is the number of years one expects to live. In other words, PA is the extent to which an individual's expectations and plans for later life have already occurred.

Melges had no similar concept, but his note that, "once hopelessness blocks the future, the risk of suicide is high,"[167] can be better understood in the light of my concept of "psychological age." When hopelessness blocks the future and a person has nothing new to expect, the Realization will be equal to 1.00 (100%) and, psychologically, a person dies: PA = (R x L = 1.0 x L) = L, means "psychological age is equal to subjectively expected longevity" or "psychological death" – the last step to suicide. In such cases, time-oriented therapy may be beneficial.

Select Bibliography

I have listed here only the writings that have been most relevant in the making of this book. It is not an exhaustive source of all the works I have consulted, though many of these are found in the Endnotes. This listing does include the major research studies both my colleagues and I have undertaken and the readings I have used to formulate my ideas. Many works are cited in Russian, and I have done my best to translate their titles for the convenience of the reader.

Akhmerov, R.A., E.I. Golovakha, E.G. Zlobina, A.A. Kronik, and D.A. Leontiev. eds. *Vremya puti: issledovaniya i razmyshleniya [Travel time: Research and reflections]*. Kiev, Ukraine: Institute of Sociology of the National Academy of Sciences, 2008.

Ast, O. curation and design. *Infinite instances: Studies and images of time.* Brooklyn, NY: Mark Batty Publisher, 2011.

Bragina, N.N., and T.A. Dobrokhotova. *Funkzionalniye assimetrii cheloveka [Human functional asymmetries]*. Moscow: Meditzina, 1988.

Cottle, T.J. *Perceiving time: a psychological investigation with men and women.* NY: Wiley & Sons, 1976.

Dozorova, M.A., N.V. Koshleva, and A.A. Kronik. *Sem ya: Programma so-zialno-lichnostnogo razvitiya detej doshkolnogo vozrasta [Seven me: A Program of social and personal development for preschool children]*. 2nd ed. Moscow: ARKTI, 2008.

Einstein, A., and L. Infeld. *The evolution of physics: The growth of ideas from early concepts to relativity and quanta.* Simon and Schuster, New York: NY: 1954.

Golovakha, E.I., and A.A. Kronik. 1989. Constructive functions of psychology. *The Soviet Journal of Psychology.* 10:6, 20-32.

——. *Psikhologicheskoye vremya lichnosti [The psychological time of personality]*. 2nd ed. Moscow: Smysl, 2008.

Kronik, A.A. ed. and contributing author. *LifeLine i drugie novie metody psykhologii zhiznennogo puti [LifeLine and other new methods of life path psychology]*. Moscow, Russia: Progress-Culture, 1993.

——. Metabolicheskaya psikhoterapiya s ispolzovaniem kompyuternoy kauzometrii [Metabolic psychotherapy with computerized causometry]. In *Vremya puti: issledovaniya i razmyshleniya,* edited by R.A. Akhmerov, E.I. Golovakha, E.G. Zlobina, A.A. Kronik, and D.A. Leontiev. Kiev, Ukraine: Institute of Sociology of the National Academy of Sciences, 2008.

Kronik, A.A., and R.A. Akhmerov. *Kauzometriya: Metody samopoznaniya, psikhodiagnostiki i psikhoterapii v psikhologii zhiznennogo puti [Causometry: Methods of self-knowledge, psychodiagnostics, and psychotherapy.]* 2nd ed. Moscow, Russia: Smysl, 2008.

Kronik, A.A., R.A. Akhmerov, and A. Speckhard. 1999. Trauma and disaster as life disrupters: A model of computer-assisted psychotherapy applied to adolescent victims of the Chernobyl disaster. *Profesional Psychology: Research and Practice,* 30: 586-599.

Kronik, A.A., E.I. Golovakha, A.L. Pajitnov, and M.A. Chlenov. *Skol'ko vam let? Linii zhizni glazami psikhologa [How old are you? The Lines of life from the psychologist's point of view].* Moscow, Russia: School Press, 1993.

Kronik, A.A., and E.A. Kronik. *Psikhologiya chelovecheskikh otnoshenij [Psychology of human relationships].* 2nd ed. Dubna, Russia: Fenix, 1998.

Kronik, A., A. Pajitnov, and B. Levin. *LifeLook® Professional Edition.* Computer software. Bethesda, MD: LifeLook.Net, 2013.

Kundera, M. *Immortality.* New York, NY: HarperCollins. 1991.

Lewin, K. *A Dynamic theory of personality.* NY: McGraw-Hill 1935.

Melges, F.T. *Time and the inner future: A temporal approach to psychiatric disorders.* NY: Wiley & Sons. 1982.

Moreno, J.L. *Who shall survive?* Washington: Nervous and Mental Disease Publishing Company, 1934.

Moskvin, V.A., and N.V. Moskvina. Funkzionalnaya assimetriya i individualnye osobennosti psikhologicheskogo vremeni cheloveka [Functional asymmetry and individual features of psychological time]. In *Vremya puti: issledovaniya i razmyshleniya,* edited by R.A. Akhmerov, E.I. Golovakha, E.G. Zlobina, A.A. Kronik, and D.A. Leontiev. Kiev, Ukraine: Institute of Sociology of the National Academy of Sciences, 2008.

Zimbardo, P.G., and J. Boyd. *The time paradox: the new psychology of time that will change your life.* NY: Free Press, 2008.

Sources

Chapters in this book are based on the following works:

Chapter 1
Kronik, A.A., and E.I. Golovakha. 1984. Psikhologicheskoe vremia: chuvstvo vozrasta [Psychological time: the sense of age]. *Znanie Sila*, 3: 20-22.
——. Skolko vam let? [How old are you?], in *Sputnik: Digest of the Soviet Press*, 12: 70-73 with translation in Australia, Austria, Belgium, Canada, Denmark, Dutch, Finland, Germany, Great Britain, Japan, New Zealand, Pakistan, Singapore, Sri Lanka, Sweden, USA. 1984.
——. The Inner sense of age. In *Infinite instances: Studies and images of time*, edited by O. Ast. NY: Mark Batty. 2011.

Chapter 2
Golovakha, E.I., and A.A. Kronik. 1983. Psikhologicheskoe vremia: paradoksy nastoyashchego [Psychological time: the paradoxes of the present]. *Znanie Sila*, 9: 27-28.

Chapter 3
Golovakha, E.I., and A.A. Kronik. 1983. Psikhologicheskoe vremia: udivitelnie svojstva szhimatsia i preriryvatsia [Psychological time: its amazing possibilities of contraction and suspension]. *Znanie Sila*, 11: 19-21.

Chapter 4
Kronik, A.A., and E.I. Golovakha. 1984. Psikhologicheskoe vremia: puteshestvia v davno i neskoro [Psychological time: the trip to long ago and not soon]. *Znanie Sila*, 2: 33-34.

Chapter 5
Golovakha, E.I., and A.A. Kronik. 1984. Tvorcheskoe dolgoletie: ot chego ono zavisit? [Creative longevity: what does it depend on]. *Nauka i Tekhnika*, 6: 28-29.

Chapter 6

Golovakha, E.I., and A.A. Kronik. 1988. Sebe i drugim: psikhologia sa-mosovershenstvovania [Wishes for myself, wishes for others: the psychology of self-improvement]. *Znanie Sila*, 4: 55-57.

———. Sebe i drugim: psikhologia samosovershenstvovania [Wishes for myself, wishes for others: the psychology of self-improvement], in *Sputnik: Digest of the Soviet Press*, 5: 100-104 with translation in Australia, Austria, Belgium, Canada, Denmark, Dutch, Finland, Germany, Great Britain, Japan, New Zealand, Pakistan, Singapore, Sri Lanka, Sweden, USA. 1989.

Chapter 7

Kronik, A.A., and B.M. Levin. *Psikhologicheskaya programma LifeLine®: Biograficheskie testy i meditatsii [Psychological software program LifeLine®: Biographical tests and meditations]*. Moscow: ParaGraph. 1991.

Kronik, A.A., A.L. Pajitnov, and B.M. Levin. LifeLine – biograficheskie testy i meditatsii za personalnym kompyuterom [LifeLine – biographic tests and meditations at the personal computer]. In *LifeLine i drugie novie metody psikhologii zhiznennogo puti*, edited by A.A. Kronik, 15-42. Moscow, Russia: Progress-Culture. 1993.

Kronik, A.A., and R.A. Akhmerov. *Kauzometriya: Metody samopoznaniya, psikhodiagnostiki i psikhoterapii v psikhologii zhiznennogo puti [Causometry: Methods of self-knowledge, psychodiagnostics, and psychotherapy]*, 136-149. Moscow, Russia: Smysl. 2008.

Kronik, A.A. 2004. *Guidebook to Personal LifeLook®*. Bethesda, MD: Life-Look.Net. http://lifelook.net/GUIDEBOOK.pdf (accessed February 15, 2016).

Chapter 8

Kronik, A.A., and R.A. Akhmerov. LifeLine v shkole, ili kak pomoch detiam spravitsia s udarami sud'by [LifeLine at school: how to help Chernobyl's children to cope with their stress]. In *LifeLine i drugie novie metody psykhologii zhiznennogo puti*, edited by A.A. Kronik, 43-59. Moscow, Russia: Progress-Culture. 1993.

Kronik, A.A., R.A. Akhmerov, and A. Speckhard. 1999. Trauma and disaster as life disrupters: A Model of computer-assisted psychotherapy applied to adolescent victims of the Chernobyl disaster. *Professional Psychology: Research and Practice*, 30: 586-599.

———. Trauma and disaster as life disrupters: A Model of computer-assisted psychotherapy applied to adolescent victims of the Chernobyl disaster. In *Chernobyl: The Event and The Aftermath*, edited by N. J. Berkowitz, and M. N. Patrick, 181-214. Madison, WI: Friends of Chernobyl Center U.S. 2001.

Kronik, A.A., and R.A. Akhmerov. *Kauzometriya: Metody samopoznaniya, psikhodiagnostiki i psikhoterapii v psikhologii zhiznennogo puti* [*Causometry: Methods of self-knowledge, psychodiagnostics, and psychotherapy*]. 2nd ed., 201-217. Moscow: Smysl, 2008.

Chapter 9

Kronik, A.A., and A.L. Pajitnov. 1986. *Biographer* [Computer software]. Moscow: Oscord.

——. Poznaj sebia cherez komp'uter [Know yourself by a computer]. *Tekhnika Molodezhi*, 6: 45-57. 1988.

Chapter 10

Kronik, A.A., and N. Orlowek. Causometry, lech lecha challenge and cognitive modifiability: How to build a bridge from the psychological past to the future. In *The Jerusalem International Conference on Neuroplasticity and Cognitive Modifiability* (*Abstracts*), 58. The Feuerstein Institute and Heronimus Markin Enterprise. June, 2013.

Kronik, A.A. Causometry, lech lecha challenge and cognitive modifiability. In *Proceedings of the Jerusalem International Conference on Neuroplasticity and Cognitive Modifiability, Jerusalem (Israel), 2-5 June 2013*, 51-55. Bologna, Italy: Medimond, 2013.

Appendix

Kronik, A.A. Definition and interpretation of LifeLine indexes. In *8th International Conference on Motivation* (*Abstracts*), edited by D.A. Leontiev, 64. Moscow: Russian State University of Humanities, June, 2002.

Notes

1   Genesis 5:5. In *Tanakh, a New translation of the holy scriptures according to the traditional Hebrew text*, NY: Jewish Publication Society, 1985.

2   S.D. Inal-Ipa, "Motivi dolgozhitelstva v Abkhazskom folklore" [Motives of longevity in Abkhazian folklore]. In *Fenomen Dolgozhitelstva: Antropologo-etnograficheskii aspect Issledovaniia*, edited by S.I. Bruk, 41-46. Moscow: Nauka, 1985.

3   D.B. Louria, H.F. Didsbury, and F. Ellerbusch. The need for a multi-level educational approach for the future. In H. F. Didsbury (Ed.) *21st Century Opportunities and Challenges: An Age of Destruction Or an Age of Transformation*, edited by H. F. Didsbury, 101. Bethesda, MD: World Future Society, 2003. See also: P.Flourens. *How to live one hundred years, clearly proved and demonstrated from practical results of the philosophers Cornado, Buffon and Cuvier*. Translated by C.Martel, 65. London: H.Bailliere Publisher, 1855.

4   Genesis 6:3.

5   Deuteronomy 34:7.

6   *Guinness world records 2018*, 69. NY: Bantam Books, 2017.

7   Nikshych, Y. *So You're an Atheist. Now What?* New York, NY: Algora Publishing, 34-35, 2015.

8   R.K. Balandin, *Vladimir Vernadsky*, 42. Moscow: MIR Publishers, 1982.

9   E.I. Golovakha and A.A. Kronik, *Psychological time of personality*, 163-164.

10 M. Zhvanetskii, *Vstrechi na ulitzach [Meetings on the streets]*. Moscow: Iskusstvo, 1980, p. 15.

11 P. Kotler, *Marketing management: Analysis, planning, implementation, and control*, 258. Upper Saddle River, NJ: Prentice Hall, 1997.

12 B. L. Neugarten, et al., "Age norms, age constraints and adult socialization." In *The Meaning of age: Selected papers of Bernice L. Neugarten*, edited by D. A. Neugarten, 26. Chicago: University of Chicago Press, 1996.

13 N.V. Panina. Sozialniy status i stil zhizni lichnosti [Social status and life style of personality]. In *Stil' zhisni lichnosti: teoreticheskie i metodologicheskie problemy, edited by* L.V. Sokhan and V.A. Tikhonovich, 286-306. Kiev, Ukraine: Naukova Dumka, 1982.

14 A.A. Kronik, and E.I. Golovakha. 1983. Psikhologichaskiy vozrast lichnosti [Psychological age of personality]. *Psikhologicheskii zhurnal,* 5: 61.

15 Kharchev, A.G., *Brak i Semya v SSSR [Marriage and family in USSR],* 204. Moscow: Mysl, 1980.

16 Epicurus, *Letter on happiness.* Translated by R. Waterfield, 21. San Francisco: Chronicle Books, 1994.

17 I. Hardi, *Vrach, sestra, bolnoi: Psikhologiia raboti s bolnimi [Physician, nurse, and patient: Psychology of patient care],* 80. Budapest: Akademiai Kiado, 1981.

18 Savich's observation, in V. Zhuravskyii, "Zolotoi Pochatok" [Golden Corn], 4. *Pravda,* November 21, 1980.

19 Antoine de Saint-Exupéry, "Letter to a hostage." In *Wartime writings 1939-1944.* Translated by N. Purcell, 114. San Diego: Harcourt Brace & Co., 1986.

20 Aristotle. *Physics.* Translated by H.G. Apostle, 85-86. Bloomington; Indiana University Press. 1969.

21 Damascius. Dubitationes et solutions in Platonis Parmenidem. In *The concept of time in late Neoplatonism: texts with translation, introduction and notes,* edited and translated by S. Sambursky, and S. Pines. 1971. Jerusalem: Israel Academy of Sciences and Humanities, 18-19, 86, 111-115. Greek text from: C.A. Ruelle, ed. *Damascius Diadochus: Dubitationes et solutiones.* Amsterdam: A.M. Hakkert, 1889/1966. See also: Damascus, the Syrian, 1889/1996. *Aporial kai lyseis peri ton proton archon, eis ton Platonos Parmeniden.* Amsterdam: Adolf M. Hakkert, 1889/1966.

22 G.S. Shlyakhtin. Razlichenie poriadka i odnovremennosti dvukh stimulov [Discrimination of sequence and simultaneousness of two stimulus]. In *Psikholofizicheskie issledovaniia,* edited by B.F. Lomov, and I.M. Zabrodin, 227-246. Moscow: Nauka, 1977.

23 J. Cohen. 1964. Psychological time. *Scientific* American, 211: 5, 118.

24 K. Lewin. *A Dynamic theory of personality,* 172-174. NY: McGraw-Hill 1935.

25 T.J. Cottle. *Perceiving time: a psychological study with men and women, 30, 46.* NY: Wiley, 1976.

26 M.S. Shaginian. *Chelovek i vremia: istoriia chelovecheskogo stanovleniia [Man and time: history of human becoming],* 297. Moscow: Khudozhestvennaia literatura. 1980.

27 J. Merlean-Ponty. 1978. Ideas of beginnings and endings in cosmology. In *The study of time III,* edited by J.T. Fraser, N. Lawrence, and D. Park, 333-369. NY: Springer.

28 L. Derbenev (Russian poet) as cited in A. Zaitsev. Past – Present – Future. *SETI League Guest Editorial,* July 2006. www.setileague.org/editor/motion.htm

29 E.I. Golovakha, and A.A. Kronik. *Psikhologichskoe vremia lichnosti*, 71-73.
30 J. Goethe. *Faust*. Translated by W.A. Kaufman, 67. Garden City, NY: Doubleday, 1961.
31 H. Reichenbach. 1924. Die Bewegungslehre bei Newton, Leibniz und Huyghens, *Kant-Studien: philosophishe Zeitschrift*, 29: 421. See also H. Reichenbach, *The Direction of time*, 25. Berkeley, UC Press, 1956.
32 L. Levy-Bruhl. *Primitive mentality*, 93. NY: Macmillan, 1923.
33 A.F. Losev. *Antichnaya filosofiia istorii* [*Ancient filosofiia of history*]. Moscow, Nauka. 1977.
34 O.M. Freidenberg. *Mif i literatura drevnosti* [*Myth and ancient literature*]. Moscow: Nauka. 1978.
35 D.S. Likhachev. *Poetica drevnerusskoi literatury* [*Poetique of ancient Russian literature*]. Moscow, Russia: Nauka, 1979.
36 M.I. Steblin-Kamenskii. *Mif* [*Myth*]. Moscow: Nauka,1976.
37 A.I. Gurevich, A.I. *Categories of medieval culture*. Boston: Routledge & Kegan Paul. 1972/1985.
38 E.I. Golovakha, and A.A. Kronik. *Psychological time of personality*, 104.
39 B.V. Zeigarnik. *Experimental abnormal psychology*, 13. NY: Plenum Press,1972.
40 E.I. Golovakha, and A.A. Kronik. *Psychological time of personality*, 68-71.
41 A.F. Losev. *Istoriia antichnoi estetiki. Ranii ellinizm* [*History of ancient aesthetics. Earliest ellynism*], 188. Moscow, Russia: Iskusstvo, 1979.
42 J. Joubert. *Some of the "thoughts" of Joseph Joubert*, 78. Boston: W.V. Spencer, 1867.
43 J. Sayen. *Einstein in America: The Scientist's conscience in the age of Hitler and Hiroshima*, 130. NY: Crown Publishers, 1985.
44 G.I. Borisovkii. Paradoksalnost' iskusstva i tochnie metody ego issledovaniia [The paradoxes of art and precise methods of their investigation]. In *Iskusstvo i tochnie nauki*, edited by A.I. Zis, 88-112. Moscow, USSR: Nauka, 1979.
45 P. Fraisse. Time in psychology. In *Time and the sciences*, edited by F. Greenaway, 71-84. Paris: UNESCO, 1979.
46 R.H. Knapp. 1960. A study of the metaphor. *Journal of Projective Techniques*, 24: 4, 389-395.
47 R.H. Knapp and J.T. Garbutt. 1958. Time imagery and the achievement motive. *Journal of Personality*, 26: 426-434.
48 Shakespeare, W. The tragedy of Hamlet, prince of Denmark, 69. NY: Washington SquarePress, 1992.
49 N.N. Bragina, and T.A. Dobrokhotova. *Funkzionalnie asymmetry cheloveka* [*Functional asymmetries in humans*]. Moscow, Russia: Medizina, 1981.
50 D.A. Granin, *Kartina* [*A picture*], 283. Leningrad, Russia: Sov. pisatel, 1980.

51 I. Kant. 1966. Antropologiia s pragmaticheskoi tochki zreniia [Anthropology from the pragmatic point of view]. In I. Kant, *Collection of works in six volumes* 6: 335-588. Moscow: Mysl.

52 J-M. Guyau 1890/1988. The origin of the idea of time. In *Guyau and the idea of time*, edited by J.A. Michon, V. Pouthas, and J.L. Jackson, 93-148. Amsterdam: North-Holland.

53 W. James. *The principles of psychology*, 408. Chicago: University of Chicago Press. 1890/1952.

54 E.I. Golovakha, and A.A. Kronik. *Psychological time of personality*, 143, 154-155.

55 Lewin's observation as cited in B.V. Zeigarnik. *Teoriia lichnosti Kurta Levina* [Kurt Lewin's theory of personality], 60. Moscow: Moscow University, 1981.

56 *The Dhammapada*, translated by S. Radhakrishnan, 167. London: Oxford University Press, 1950.

57 N.K. Rerikh. *Iz literaturnogo naslediia [From literature heritage]*, 396, Moscow: Izobrazitelnoe iskusstvo, 1974.

58 T.J. Cottle. *Perceiving time: a psychological investigation with men and women*, 85-91. NY: Wiley & Sons, 1976.

59 E.I. Golovakha, and A.A. Kronik. *Psychological time of personality*. 143, 158.

60 E.S. Kuzmin. Personal communication at the meeting of the Conference of Young Psychologists, Obninsk, Russia. Fall, 1981.

61 T.J. Cottle. *Perceiving time*. 105.

62 E.I. Golovakha, and A.A. Kronik. *Psychological time of personality*. 118-119.

63 S. Freud. Repression. In *The standard edition of the complete psychological works of Sigmund Freud* 14: 140-158, edited by J. Strachey. London: Hogarth Press. 1915/1963.

64 A. Jersild. 1931. Memory for the pleasant as compared with the unpleasant. *Journal of Experimental Psychology*, 14:3, 284-288.

65 N.D. Weinstein. 1980. Unrealistic optimism about future life events. *Journal of Personality and Social Psychology*, 39:5, 806-820.

66 R. Krafft-Ebing. *An experimental study in the domain of hypnotism*. NY: Putnam. 1888

67 O.K. Tikhomirov, V.L. Raikov, and N.A. Berezanskaya. 1975. Ob odnom podkhode k issledovaniu mishleniia kak deiatelnosti lichnosti [An approach to study cognitive process as activity of personality]. In *Psychologicheskie issledovania tvorcheskoi deiatelnosti*, edited by O.K. Tikhomirov, 143-204. Moscow, Russia: Nauka.

68 H. Bergson. *Matter and memory*, Mineola, N.Y.: Dover. 1908/2004. See also H. Mann, M. Siegler, and H. Osmond. 1971. The psychotypol-

ogy of time. In *The future of time: Man's temporal environment,* edited by H. Yaker, H. Osmond, and F. Cheek. 142-178. Garden City, N.Y.: Doubleday. See also Zimbardo and Boyd's *The Time paradox.*

69 A.I. Rabin. 1978. Future time perspective and ego strength. In *The Study of time III,* edited by J.T. Fraser, N. Lawrence, and D. Park, 294-306. NY: Springer.

70 O. Wilde. *The Picture of Dorian Gray, 204.* NY: Modern Library, 1992.

71 A.A. Kronik, and E.A. Kronik. *V glavnykh rolyakh: vy, my, on, ty, ya. Psikhologiya znachimykh otnoshenij [The cast of characters: thou, they, we, you, me. The psychology of significant relationships],* 10. Moscow: Mysl. 1989.

72 Other translations from the Russian in V.I. Vysotsky. 1972/2000. I love you now. *Speaking in Tongues: The Magazine of Literary Translation* www.spintongues.msk.ru/vysotsky3.htm:
I love you now, in fact,
And I don't hold it back.
It's not "before," not "after"
– your rays set me afire.
Whether I weep or I smile
I love you in this while,
the future I don't want, the past I don't desire.

73 F.I. Tyutchev. K.B. *Poems & political letters of F.I. Tyutchev,* 117. Knoxville: UT Press, 1870/1973.

74 E. Zola as cited in S.O. Gruzenberg, *Geniy i tvorchestvo: osnovi teorii i psikhologii tvorchestva [Genius and creativity: foundations of the theory and psychology of creativity],* 96. Leningrad, Russia: Soikin, 1924.

75 Pin-hsin. *Fansin [Twinkling stars],* 9. Shanghai, China: The Commercial Press Ltd. 1923/1930. Cited poem was translated by Diana Chen, Reference Librarian, Asian Division, Library of Congress, August 23, 2012.

76 N.N. Bragina, and T.A. Dobrokhotova, *Functional asymmetries.* 112-144.

77 M. Leeds. 1944. One form of paramnesia: The illusion of déjà vu. *The Journal of the American Society for Psychical Research,* 38:1, 24-42. See also: V.M. Neppe. *The psychology of déjà vu: have I been here before?* Johannesburg: Witwatersrand Univ. Press, 1983. See also: J. Janson. *Das Déjà vuerlebnis.* Frankfurt am Main, NY: P. Lang. 1991.

78 I.A. Goncharov. *Oblomov,* 287. Cambridge, MA. R. Bentley, 1915/1979.

79 Friedman's, Bradley's, Oakden's and Sturt's studies as cited in A.T. Jersild, J.S. Brook, and D.W. Brook. *The psychology of adolescence,* 157. NY: Macmillan, 1978.

80 Ö. Sande. 1972. Future consciousness. *Journal of Peace Research,* 3: 271-278.

81 G. de Maupassant. *Bel-Ami,* 161. Harmondsworth, Penguin, 1975.

82 V. Skirbekk. *Age and individual productivity: a literature survey*, 36. Max Planck Institute for Demographic Research, 2003.

83 H.C. Lehman. *Age and achievement*. Princeton: Princeton Univ. Press, 1953. See also: H.C. Lehman 1968. The creative production rates of present versus past generations of scientists. In *Middle age and aging: a reader in social psychology*, edited by B.L. Neugarten, 99-105. Chicago: Univ. of Chicago Press.

84 V. Shklovskiy. 2002. Pisma k vnuku [Letters to grandson]. *Voprosy Literatury*, 4: 264-300.

85 Rudkevich's study as cited in M.D. Aleksandrova. 1974. *Problemy sotsial'noi i psikhologicheskoi gerontologii [Problems of social and psychological gerontology]*, 108-115. Leningrad, Russia: Leningradskii Univ.

86 *The Dhammapada*, 141.

87 A.A. Kronik. 1985. Kartina produktivnosti zhizni i ee dinamika v samosoznanii lichnosti [Image of life productivity and its subjective dynamics]. In *Zhizn kak tvorchestvo*, edited by L.V. Sokhan, 265-277. Kiev, Ukraine: Naukova Dumka.

88 G. de Maupassant. *Bel-Ami*, 161. Harmondsworth, Penguin, 1975.

89 A. Herzen, A. *My past and thoughts*, 64. Berkeley: UC Press. 1982.

90 Over 30 and over the hill. *The Economist*, June 24, 2004.

91 H. Hesse. *Steppenwolf*, 51. Westport, CN. Ltd. Ed. Club, 1928/1977.

92 E.I. Golovakha, and A.A. Kronik, *Wishes for myself, wishes for others*, 55-57.

93 K. Gibran. *Sand and Foam*, 38. New Delhi: Sterling, 1926/2009.

94 www.lifelook.net/catalog.html

95 I.S. Klochkov. *Dukhovnaya kultura Vavilonii: chelovek, sud'ba, vremya [The spiritual culture of Babylon: man, fate, time]*. Moscow: Nauka, 1983.

96 R. Wilhelm, and C.A. Baynes. *The I Ching or Book of Changes*. Princeton, NJ: Princeton University Press. 1967.

97 G. de Maupassant. *Bel-Ami*, 161.

98 H. Selye. *Stress without distress*, 109. NY: J. B. Lippincott Co. 1974.

99 C. Linnaei. 1758. Systema naturae per regna tria naturae, secundum classes, ordines, genera, species, cum characteribus, differentiis, synonymis, locis. Tomus I. 10th ed. Holmiae: Impensis Direct, Laurentii Salvii, 20.

100 A.A.Kronik, R.A. Akhmerov, and A. Speckhard. 1999. Trauma and disaster as life disrupters: A Model of computer-assisted psychotherapy applied to adolescent victims of the Chernobyl disaster. *Professional Psychology: Research and Practice*, 30: 586-599.

101 A.A. Kronik, B.M. Levin, and A.L. Pajitnov. *LifeLine®: The biographical tests and meditations* [Computer software]. Moscow: ParaGraph. 1991.

102 R. Janoff-Bulman. *Shattered assumptions: Towards a new psychology of trauma*. NY: The Free Press, 1992.

103 Meyerson, M. 1995. Psychological consequences of the nuclear accident in Chernobyl. *IODA Journal*, 3: 27-30. Roche, A. 1996. *Children of Chernobyl: The Human cost of the world's worst nuclear disaster*. London: Harper Collins. See also O. Yakovenko, 1996. Psykhichnyi stan lyudey ta psykhologichna dopomoga u postchernobylskiy sytuazii [Psychological status of people and psychological support in the post-Chernobyl situation]. In *Sozialni naslidky chornobylskoi katastrofy: resultaty soziologichnyh doslidzhen 1986-1995 rokiv [Social consequences of the Chernobyl catastrophe: Results of sociological polls in 1986-1995]*, edited by V.M. Vorona, E.I. Golovakha, and Y. I. Sayenko, 354-367. Kharkow: Folio.

104 I.Z. Holowinsky. 1993. Chernobyl nuclear catastrophe and the high risk potential for mental retardation. *Mental Retardation*, 31: 35-40.

105 S.J. Kaplan. 1968. Radiation. In *International Encyclopedia of the Social Sciences*, 13: 290-294. NY: Macmillan.

106 L.N. Astakhova, L.R. Anspaugh, G.W. Beebe, A. Bouville, V.V. Drosdovitch, V. Garber, Y.I. Gavrilin, V.T. Khrough, A.V. Kuvshinnikov, Y.N. Kuzmenkov, V.P. Minenko, K.V. Moschik, A.S. Nalivko, J. Robbins, E.V. Shemiakina, S. Shinkarev, S.I. Tochitskaya, and M.A. Waclawiw. 1998. Chernobyl-related thyroid cancer in children of Belarus: A Case-control study. *Radiation Research*, 150: 349-356. See also V.A. Stsjazhko, A.F. Tsyb, N.D. Tronko, G. Souchkevitch, and K.F. Baverstock. 1995. Childhood thyroid cancer since accident at Chernobyl. *British Medical Journal*, 310: 801.

107 V.S. Koscheyev, G.R. Leon, A.V. Gourine, and V.N. Gourine. 1997. The psychosocial aftermath of the Chernobyl disaster in an area of relatively low contamination. *Prehospital and Disaster Medicine*, 12: 41-46. See also E.J. Bromet, G. Carlson, D. Goidgaber, and S. Gluzman. Health effects of the Chernobyl catastrophe on mothers and children. In *Toxic contamination: The Interface of psychological and physical health effects*, presented at the XIV annual meeting of the International Society for Traumatic Stress Studies, Washington, D.C. 1998.

108 V. Nestorenko. Total body radiation in a sample of 6000 Belarusian children. Paper presented at the International Symposium on Assessing the Impact on Mothers and Children of Living in the Ecocide Zones, Minsk, Belarus. October, 1997.

109 B.L. Green, J.D. Lindy, and M.C. Grace. 1994. Psychological effects of toxic contamination. In *Individual and community responses to trauma and disaster: The structure of human chaos, edited by R. J. Ursano, B.G. McCaughey & C.S. Fullerton*. 154-176. Cambridge: Cambridge Univ. Press. See also B.L. Green, 1998. Psychological responses to disasters:

Conceptualization and identification of high-risk survivors. *Psychiatry and Clinical Neurosciences*, 52S, 67-73.

110 Ibid.

111 E.J. Bromet. 1995. Methodological issues in designing research on community-wide disasters with special reference to Chernobyl. In *Extreme Stress and Communities: Impact and Intervention*, edited by S. E. Hobfoll, and M.W. de Vries, 267-282. Dordrecht: Kluwer Academic Publishers.

112 M.I. Bobneva, ed. *Chernobylskiy sled: postradavshie deti* [*Chernobyl trace: the children who suffered*]. Moscow: Votum-psy. 1992. See also M.R. Kidd, 1991. The children of Chernobyl. *The Medical Journal of Australia*, 155: 764-767. See also A. Roche. *Children of Chernobyl: The Human Cost of the World's Worst Nuclear Disaster*. London: HarperCollins Publishers. 1996.

113 A.A. Kronik, B.M. Levin, and A.L. Pajitnov. *LifeLine®: The biographical tests and meditations* [Computer software]. Moscow: ParaGraph. 1991.

114 E.I. Golovakha, and A.A. Kronik. *Psychological time of Personality.*

115 The term, "domain" refers to various areas of life such as family life, business life, inner life, social life, physical health, and experience with nature.

116 M. Lusher, and I.A. Scott. *The Lusher color test*. NY: Pocket Books. 1971.

117 Motivational status refers to the way a person has indicated (analyzed) goals and causal connections between pairs of events. The number and strength of connections any event has with other events are measures of how much this event influences the other; that is, how much it motivates his or her life.

118 B. Van der Kolk. 1994. The body keeps the score: memory and the evolving psychobiology of posttraumatic stress. *Harvard Review of Psychiatry*, 1:5, 253-265.

119 ibid.

120 E.I. Golovakha. *Zhiznennaya perspectiva i professionalnoye samoopredelenie molodezhi* [*Life prospects and professional self-determination of young people*]. Kiev: Naukova Dumka. 1988.

121 L. Lerner. 1991. Proshedshiy skvoz stenu [Going through the wall]. *Ogonek*, 3: 22-24.

122 Each participant was instructed to estimate on a scale of 0-9 (0 = minimum eventfulness; 9 = maximum eventfulness) how eventful each five-year period of his or her life had been in the past, and is predicted to be in the future. We call the resulting bar graph, in which years of a person's life form the horizontal axis and degree of eventfulness is the vertical axis, a life graph in the LifeLook program.

123 A. Blok as cited in M. Guerman, *Vasily Kandinsky*, 106. London, UK: Parkstone International, 2015.

124 In this context, psychological age is operationally defined as equal to the product of realization x years that one expects to live. Realization equals the ratio of the psychological past (one's memories) to the sum of the whole. The formula is PA = R x L, where PA is psychological age, R is realization, and L is the number of years one expects to live. In other words, psychological age can be measured by the extent to which an individual's expectations and plans for later life have already taken place.

125 A.A. Kronik. 1993. *LifeLine i drugie novye metody psikhologii zhiznennogo puti [LifeLine and other new methods of psycho-biographical analysis]*, 55-59. Moscow: Progress-Culture. See also: R.A. Akhmerov, 2014. Changes in Subjective Picture of Life Path after Biographic Training. *Journal of Siberian Federal University. Humanities and Social Sciences*, 7:12, 2137-2144.

126 American Psychiatric Association. 1994. *Diagnostic and statistical manual of mental disorders*, 4th ed. Washington, D.C.: Author.

127 R. Janoff-Bulman. *Shattered Assumptions*.

128 I.L. McCann, and L.A. Pearlman. 1992. Constructivist self-development theory: a theoretical framework for assessing and treating traumatized college students. *Journal of American College Health*, 40: 189-196.

129 A.A. Kronik, and R.A. Akhmerov. 1988. Motivatsionnaya nedostatochnost kak kriteriy deformirovannosti sub'ektivnoy kartiny zhiznennogo puti [Motivational deficiency as a criteria for deformation of the subjective life picture]. In *Motivatzionnaya regulyatsiya deyatelnosti i povedeniya cheloveka [Motivational regulation of individual activity and behavior]*, edited by L. I. Anziferova, 136-140. Moscow: Institute of Psychology. See also R.A. Akhmerov. Biograficheskie krizisy lichnosti [Biographical crises of personality]. PhD diss, Institute of Psychology, Moscow, Russia 1994.

130 Thai Chi Sung. Samootsenka psikhologicheskogo vozrasta [The Self-estimation of the psychological age]. PhD diss, Saint Petersburg Univ, Russia. 1991.

131 E.I. Golovakha, and N. Panina. 1996. Konzeptualni zasady vymiryuvannya sozialnogo samopochuttia ta psykhologichnogo stanu poterpilogo naselennya i postchornobylska sozialna polityka [Conceptual basis for measuring of the social self-feeling and psychological status of a victimized population and post-Chernobyl social policy]. In *Sozialni naslidky chornobylskoi katastrofy: resultaty soziologichnyh doslidzhen 1986-1995 rokiv [Social consequences of the Chernobyl catastrophe: results of sociological polls in 1986-1995]*, edited by V.M. Vorona, E. I. Golovakha, and Y.I. Sayenko. 51-56. Kharkow: Folio.

132 V.S. Khomik, and A.A. Kronik. 1988. Otnoshenie k vremeni: psikhologicheskie problemy ranney alkogolizatsii i otkloniayushchego

povedenia [Attitude to time: psychological aspects of early alcohol-addiction and of deviant behavior]. *Voprosy Psikhologii*, 1: 98-106. (This research was conducted in 1984). See also Blokhin, K.N., and A.A. Kronik. 2006. Distortions of psychological time in patients with opioid dependence. *4th Biennial International Conference on Personal Meaning: Addiction, Meaning & Spirituality*, 50-51. Vancouver, Canada: International Network on Personal Meaning; Blokhin, K.N., and A.A. Kronik. *Disturbances of time experience in patients with opioid dependence*, http://lifelook.net/distortionsintime.pdf. Accessed January 1, 2006.

133 S. Yakovenko, ed. *Psikhologicheskaya pomoshch detiam Chernobylia [Psychological support for Chernobyl's children]*. Kiev: Institute of Psychology. 1990.

134 E.I. Golovakha. 1996. Dynamika psykhologichnogo stanu likvidatoriv [Dynamic of psychological status of liquidators]. In *Sozialni naslidky chornobylskoi katastrofy: resultaty sociologichnyh doslidzhen 1986-1995 rokiv [Social consequences of the Chernobyl catastrophe: results of sociological polls in 1986-1995]*, edited by V.M. Vorona, E. I. Golovakha and Y.I. Sayenko, 308-317. Kharkow: Folio. See also A.V. Kondrashev and A.A. Kronik, 1991. Psycho-biographical analysis with APL. *APL Quote Quad*, 21: 244-248.

135 M. Rahu, M. Tekkel, and T. Veidebaum. 1997. The Estonian study of Chernobyl cleanup workers II: Incidence of cancer and mortality. *Radiation Research*, 147: 653-657.

136 O. Yakovenko, 1996. Psykhichnyi stan lyudey ta psykhologichna dopomoga u postchernobylskiy sytuazii [Psychological status of people and psychological support in the post-Chernobyl situation]. In *Sozialni naslidky chornobylskoi katastrofy: resultaty soziologichnyh doslidzhen 1986-1995 rokiv* [Social consequences of the Chernobyl catastrophe: results of sociological polls in 1986-1995], edited by V.M. Vorona, E.I. Golovakha, and Y.I. Sayenko, 354-367. Kharkow: Folio.

137 R.A. Akhmerov. 1993. Biograficheskiy trening pri krizisah serediny zhizni [Biographical training for middle-life crisis]. In *LifeLine i drugie-novye metody psikhologii zhiznennogo puti [LifeLine and others new methods of psycho-biographical analysis]*, edited by A.A. Kronik, 140-151. Moscow: Progress-Culture. See also R.A. Akhmerov, Biograficheskie krizisy lichnosti [Biographical crises of personality]. PhD diss, Institute of Psychology, Moscow, Russia. 1994.

138 J. Brier. *Psychological assessment of adult posttraumatic states*. Washington, DC: American Psychological Association. 1997. See also C.S. Fullerton, and R.J. Ursano, eds. *Posttraumatic stress disorder: acute and long-term responses to trauma and disaster*. Washington, DC: American Psychiatric Press. 1997. See also J.L. Herman. *Trauma and recovery: The Aftermath of violence: From domestic abuse to political terror*. NY: Basic Books. 1992.

139 N. Koreneva. March 20, 1985. Muzika visokoi pravdy. Puteshestvie po "komnate Rikhtera" [Music of the high truth. Trip to the "Rikhter's room"]. *Komsomolskaia Pravda*, 4.

140 G.O. Neugarten, and G.O. Hagestad. 1976. Age and the life course. In *Handbook of aging and the social sciences*, edited by R. H. Binstock and E. Shanas, 35-55, NY, Litten.

141 O.M.Tkachenko, and A.A. Kronik, 1973. Pro spezyfiku mekhanizmu sozialnoi determinatzii psykhichnykh yavyshch [Specifity of social determination of psychological phenomena]. *Problemy Filosofii*, 27, 41-43. Kiev, Ukraine: Kiev University.

142 E.I. Golovakha, and A.A. Kronik, 1989. Constructive functions of psychology. *The Soviet Journal of Psychology: A cover-to-cover translation of Psikhologicheskii Zhurnal*, 10:6, 20-32.

143 A.A. Kronik, A. Pajitnov and B. Levin. *LifeLook® Professional Edition*.

144 A.A. Kronik, and R.A. Akhmerov, *Causometry: Methods of self knowledge*.

145 E.I. Golovakha, and A.A. Kronik. *Psychological time of personality*.

146 Genesis 12:1.

147 A.A. Kronik, 1993. Metabolicheskaya psikhoterapiya s ispolzovaniem kompyuternoy kauzometrii [Metabolic psychotherapy with computerized causometry]. In *Vremya puti: Issledovaniya i razmyshleniya [Travel time: Research and reflections]*, edited by R.A.Akhmerov et al, 91-113. Kiev, Ukraine: Institute of Sociology of the National Academy of Sciences.

148 A.A. Kronik, R.A. Akhmerov, and A. Speckhard. *Trauma and disaster as life disrupters*.

149 N.N. Bragina, and T.A. Dobrokhotova. *Functional asymmetries*. See also V.A. Moskvin, and N.V. Moskvina, *Functional asymmetry and individual features of psychological time*.

150 V.V. Gavrilov, and A.A. Kronik. O prostranstvennoy sinkhronizatsii medlennikh potentsialov mozga pri vospominaniyakh i predstavlenii budushchego [Spacial synchronization of brain slow potentials during remembering and imaginatio of the future]. Paper presented at the 4th All-Union Meeting on Modeling and Methods of Analysis of Brain Bioelectrical Activity, Pushchino, Russia, April 1991. See also V.V. Gavrilov. 1992. Brain slow potentials during remembering and imagination of subjectively significant life's events. *International Journal of Psychology*, 27: 414.

151 M. Kundera. *Immortality*, 226-227. New York; NY, 1991.

152 S. Paige as cited in G. Leinwand. 2010. *Intimations of immortality: Do you want to live forever?* IX. Bloomington, IN: AuthorHouse, 2010.

153 H. Yakobson. *Crossing borders: From revolutionary Russia to China to America*. Tenafly, NJ: Hermitage Publishers, 1994.

154 A.A. Kronik, A. Pajitnov and B. Levin. *LifeLook® Professional Edition.*
155 E.I. Golovakha, and A.A. Kronik. *Psychological time of personality.*
156 F.T. Melges. 1982. *Time and the inner future: A temporal approach to psychiatric disorders.* NY: Wiley & Sons.
157 Ibid, 144.
158 Ibid, 295.
159 Ibid, 173, 197, 215.
160 Ibid, 297.
161 Ibid, 294, 141.
162 Ibid, 225.
163 Ibid, 221.
164 Ibid, 222.
165 American Psychiatric Association. *Diagnostic and statistical manual of mental disorders,* 32.
166 F.T. Melges. *Time and the inner future,* 134.
167 Ibid, 177.

About the Author

Aleksandr A. Kronik received his Ph.D. and Sc.D. in psychology (1979, 1995), both from the Russian Academy of Sciences, Institute of Psychology. He coined the term "Causometry," for measuring the goal-and-causal connections between life events, so people could better understand their life visions, and change them when desired.

He is the author/co-author of eight books:
Interpersonal Perception in Small Groups (1982)
Psychological Time of Personality (1984/2008)
Psychology of Significant Relationships (1989/1998)
How Old Are You? The lines of life from the psychologist's point of view (1993)
LifeLine and Other New Methods of Life Path Psychology (1993)
Some Archival Sources for Ukrainian-Jewish Genealogy (1998)
Causometry: Methods of Self-knowledge, Psychodiagnostics, and Psychotherapy (2003/2008)
Seven Me: A program of social and personal development for preschool children (2005/2008)

Dr. Kronik is currently a licensed psychologist and maintains an independent practice in the Washington DC area, doing clinical work, research and consulting. He has treated numerous patients, using his causograms and other causal and goal-based tools for improving lives.

Acknowledgments

I am blessed by the longtime friendship of my colleagues and co-authors. The theory of psychological time and causometry were developed in collaboration with Dr. Eugene Golovakha, Ph.D., Sc.D., at the Ukrainian Academy of Sciences Institute of Philosophy (Kiev). LifeLook software (aka LifeLine in Russia) was created in a Dream Team that included Alexey Pajitnov and Boris Levin at the Russian-American Company "ParaGraph" (Moscow). Time-oriented psychotherapy was developed in the creative dialogues with Dr. Rashad Akhmerov, Ph.D., at the Russian Academy of Sciences and Dr. Anne Speckhard, Ph.D., from Georgetown University (Washington, DC).

I am indebted to my new colleagues and clinical mentors in the United States—Drs. John Breeskin, Harvey L. P. Resnik, and Sallyann Amdur Sack—who helped the idea of this book to settle on American soil, in spite of our differences in languages and cultures.

My appreciation to Prof. Helen B. Yakobson, from the George Washington University, for sponsoring translations from Russian, and Olga Ast, Diana Chen, Roseli Ejzenberg, Barbara E. Kaplan, Hilary LaMonte, Morton Leeds, Llyid Muller, Lisa F. Orenstein, Nathaniel Orlowek, Mary Radnofsky, Alexander Semenov, Mikhail Shishkin, Sherry Spector, Dr. Sheri A. Wilson for their translations and editorial help, as well as to Alexandr Dozorov and Oleg Gershunskiy for their programming work, and Vicki McGill and Larry Paine for their artwork.

Ideas presented in this popular book have been helpful to many people in different countries in good and bad times – this is very inspiring to the author. I hope you too, as a new reader, will find them helpful in your search to live your own life in a healthier, happier, and more productive way. Special thanks to the brave Swedish actor Peter Stormare, from the Royal Dramatic Theater, who was one of the first to use LifeLook in Moscow in the 20th century, and the curious Potomac reader and good friend Danny Penini, from D&F Construction, who tirelessly encouraged me to publish this book in the 21st.

Very special thanks to my dear wife and our children for practical help and unconditional support during my many years of being puzzled by "How Young Are You?"

For permission to reprint with adaptations the materials in Chapter 8, I thank the editors of the journal, *Professional Psychology: Research and Practice*, with respect to "Trauma and Disaster: A Model of Computer-Assisted Psychotherapy Applied to Adolescent Victims of the Chernobyl Disaster", by A. A. Kronik et al, Volume 30, pp. 586-599, copyright 1999 by the American Psychological Association. This clinical research was supported in part by a grant from the Ukrainian Chernobyl Department and the Ukrainian Institute of Psychology.

Finally, my deep gratitude to Rabbi Joel Tessler and Rabbi Yaakov Benamou for their inspirational feedback and to Anna Lawton, the founder of New Academia Publishing, for her timeless encouragement and great patience during a dozen years while a manuscript grew up into the book.

...With the help of the divine sparks in each of these and many other wonderful individuals, who are illuminating the lines of my life.

Let's Continue with Brainstorming

**Ten Questions to a Future Colleague
on the Study of Time and Causometry Research**

How can the paradoxes of psychological age and time be resolved?

How can we measure the significance of life events and wisdom?

How do we categorize life events? Is a universal, culture-free dictionary possible?

What are the criteria for the complexity of a causogram? How can we measure complexity?

Can we develop a taxonomy of causograms for clinicians?

Are seven steps enough for effective metabolic psychotherapy or coaching?

Is the corpus callosum in charge of bridging the psychological past and future?

How can we employ causometry to reach consensus among groups of people, such as partners, families, communities, nations, and others?

Do our musical preferences somehow express or reflect the structure of our causogram?

Can we define the limits of causogram modifiability?

Visit www.LifeLook.Net...

www.ingramcontent.com/pod-product-compliance
Lightning Source LLC
Chambersburg PA
CBHW070943150426
42812CB00066B/3249/J